MEXICO

COMPREHENSIVE TRAVEL GUIDE 2024

Explore History, Culture, Hidden Gems, Cuisine and Local Secrets in the Southern portion of North America – Packed with Detailed Maps & Travel Itineraries

BY

MICHAEL VIANNEY

TABLE OF CONTENTS

CHAPTER 1
INTRODUCTION

1.1 Welcome to Mexico

Mexico is a land where vibrant traditions blend seamlessly with breathtaking landscapes, offering an experience that is both enriching and exhilarating. As you step into this diverse country, you're greeted by a symphony of colors, sounds, and flavors that promise to captivate every sense. From the bustling streets of its capital to the serene beauty of its coastal regions, Mexico invites you on a journey that will linger in your memory long after you leave. In Mexico City, the heart of the nation, you'll find yourself immersed in a whirlwind of cultural and historical marvels. The grand Zócalo, the main square, serves as a vibrant center where history and contemporary life merge. Here, you can marvel at the Metropolitan Cathedral, an architectural wonder that has stood the test of time, and the National Palace, where Diego Rivera's murals tell stories of Mexico's rich past. Just a short walk away, the ancient ruins of Templo

Mayor stand as a testament to the Aztec civilization's grandeur, offering a fascinating glimpse into a bygone era.

Traveling to the Yucatán Peninsula, the magic of Chichen Itza unfolds before you. This ancient Mayan city, with its iconic pyramid of El Castillo, is a wonder of engineering and astronomy. As you explore the site, you'll be awed by the precision of Mayan architecture and the grandeur of structures like the Temple of the Warriors and the Great Ball Court. The experience is heightened by a visit to the cenotes, natural sinkholes that are both refreshing and beautiful. Cenote Ik Kil, with its crystal-clear waters and lush vegetation, provides the perfect respite after a day of exploration. The Riviera Maya, stretching along Mexico's Caribbean coastline, is a paradise for those seeking relaxation and natural beauty. Playa del Carmen is a lively destination where you can bask in the sun on pristine beaches and dive into the clear blue waters. The energy of Quinta Avenida, with its array of shops, restaurants, and bars, offers a vibrant nightlife that complements the serene beach experience. For a quieter escape, Tulum presents a blend of history and tranquility. The ancient Mayan ruins overlooking the turquoise sea provide a stunning backdrop to the relaxed pace of the beaches, making it an ideal spot for reflection and rejuvenation. Oaxaca, with its rich cultural heritage, invites you to explore its vibrant markets and savor its renowned cuisine. Mercado Benito Juárez, a bustling market in the city center, offers a sensory overload of colors and aromas. The city's culinary scene, famous for its complex and flavorful mole, provides a delicious adventure for the palate. Nearby, the archaeological site of Monte Albán, perched on a mountaintop, offers panoramic views and insights into the early Mesoamerican civilizations that shaped the region.

In the northern state of Chihuahua, the Copper Canyon presents a dramatic landscape that rivals even the Grand Canyon. The Chihuahua al Pacífico Railway, known as El Chepe, takes you on a breathtaking journey through this vast canyon system. Each twist and turn of the track reveals new vistas, from rugged cliffs to verdant valleys. Stops along the way, such as the town of Creel, allow you to engage with the local Tarahumara people and experience their unique culture. The sheer scale and beauty of the Copper Canyon provide an unforgettable adventure for those with a love for the outdoors. Mexico is a country of contrasts and convergence, where every region offers a new adventure and every experience enriches your journey.

1.2 My Experience in Mexico

The moment my plane began its descent over Mexico City, I was captivated by the sprawling urban landscape below. The city seemed to stretch infinitely, a vibrant tapestry of colors and lights. As I stepped off the plane, I was greeted by a warm, fragrant breeze carrying the faint scent of spices and flowers. It was an invitation to adventure, a promise of rich experiences waiting to be discovered. Mexico City, the beating heart of the nation, welcomed me with open arms. My days there were a delightful blend of exploration and discovery. The historic center, with its grand colonial architecture and bustling plazas, felt like stepping back in time. The Zócalo, one of the largest city squares in the world, was a hub of activity, surrounded by the impressive Metropolitan Cathedral and the National Palace. Wandering through these streets, I was struck by the seamless blend of ancient and modern. Amidst the historic buildings, contemporary art galleries and chic cafes thrived, creating a dynamic cultural mosaic. One of the highlights of my visit was the exploration of the city's numerous museums. The National Museum of Anthropology was a treasure trove of artifacts from Mexico's pre-Columbian heritage. Each exhibit told a story of ancient civilizations, from the mysterious Olmecs to the mighty Aztecs. The murals of Diego Rivera at the Palacio de Bellas Artes left me in awe, their vibrant colors and powerful narratives capturing the essence of Mexican history and identity.

Beyond the city's historical and cultural riches, its neighborhoods offered a more intimate glimpse into local life. In Coyoacán, I strolled through charming cobblestone streets lined with colorful houses and lively markets. This area, once home to Frida Kahlo, had an artistic and bohemian vibe. Visiting the Frida Kahlo Museum, housed in her former residence, was an emotional experience. Her art, deeply personal and vividly expressive, offered a window into her soul and the tumultuous times she lived through. Food in Mexico City was an adventure in itself. From street vendors selling tacos al pastor to upscale restaurants offering modern takes on traditional dishes, every meal was a celebration of flavors. I savored the complex layers of mole, the freshness of ceviche, and the comforting warmth of a bowl of pozole. Each bite was a testament to Mexico's rich culinary heritage, a fusion of indigenous ingredients and Spanish influences.

Leaving Mexico City, I traveled to the Yucatán Peninsula, where the pace of life slowed down, and nature took center stage. The ancient Mayan ruins of Chichen Itza were awe-inspiring. Standing before the towering Pyramid of Kukulcán, I felt a profound connection to the past. The nearby cenotes, natural sinkholes filled with crystal-clear water, offered a refreshing escape from the heat. Swimming in these sacred waters, surrounded by lush vegetation and the sounds of the jungle, was a serene and rejuvenating experience. In contrast to the tranquility of the cenotes, the coastal town of Tulum was a vibrant mix of beach life and history. The ruins of the ancient Mayan port city perched on cliffs overlooking the turquoise Caribbean Sea were a breathtaking sight. As I lounged on the white sandy beaches, sipping on a cold drink and watching the waves roll in, I understood why so many travelers are drawn to this idyllic spot.

My journey in Mexico concluded in the charming city of Oaxaca, renowned for its indigenous cultures and culinary traditions. The vibrant markets, filled with the aroma of freshly ground coffee and spices, were a feast for the senses. I indulged in local delicacies like tlayudas and chapulines (grasshoppers), and marveled at the skill of artisans creating intricate textiles and pottery. The Day of the Dead celebrations in Oaxaca were particularly memorable. The city came alive with colorful altars, music, and dance, honoring ancestors in a joyous and heartfelt manner. Reflecting on my time in Mexico, I am filled with a deep appreciation for the country's rich history, diverse culture, and warm hospitality. Every moment was a new discovery, every encounter a story waiting to be told. Mexico is a land of contrasts and surprises, where ancient traditions coexist with modern innovation, and natural beauty is matched by the vibrancy of its people. My journey through Mexico was more than a trip; it was an adventure that stirred my soul and left me longing to return.

1.3 About This Guide

This guide is meticulously crafted as a travel companion designed to enrich your journey through one of the most vibrant and diverse countries in the world. Mexico is a land of contrasts, where ancient traditions blend seamlessly with modern innovation, where bustling cities coexist with serene beaches, and where every region offers a unique tapestry of culture, cuisine, and natural beauty. Whether you're a first-time visitor or a seasoned traveler, this guide will provide you with everything you need to make the most of your Mexican adventure.

Maps and Navigation: Navigating Mexico's vast landscapes and bustling urban centers can be daunting, but with the right tools, it becomes an exciting part of your adventure. This guide includes detailed maps of major cities, tourist attractions, and transportation networks. You'll find both offline (paper) maps and digital maps accessible via QR codes, ensuring you have navigation support at your fingertips, whether you're exploring the colonial streets of Guanajuato or the ancient ruins of Teotihuacan.

Accommodation Options: Mexico offers a wide range of accommodation options to suit every traveler's budget and preference. From opulent beachfront resorts in Cancun and Los Cabos to charming bed and breakfasts in Oaxaca and San Cristobal de las Casas, this guide provides detailed information on the best places to stay. Each listing includes contact information, price ranges, amenities, and insider tips to help you find the perfect home away from home.

Transportation: Traveling within Mexico is an adventure in itself. This guide covers all modes of transportation, including domestic flights, long-distance buses, car rentals, and local public transit systems. You'll learn how to navigate Mexico City's extensive metro system, find the most scenic train routes, and even get tips for driving in Mexico's diverse terrains. Additionally, practical advice on booking tickets, understanding schedules, and ensuring safety will help you travel with confidence.

Top Attractions: From the sun-soaked beaches of the Riviera Maya to the majestic pyramids of Chichen Itza, Mexico is home to countless iconic attractions. This guide highlights the must-see destinations across the country, offering historical context, visiting tips, and recommendations for making the most of your time at each site. Whether you're exploring the vibrant murals of Mexico City, snorkeling in the crystal-clear waters of Cozumel, or hiking through the Copper Canyon, you'll find all the information you need to create unforgettable memories.

Practical Information and Travel Resources: Traveling to a new country involves a lot of planning and preparation. This guide provides practical information on visa requirements, health and safety tips, currency exchange, and communication. You'll also find useful resources such as emergency contact numbers, local customs and etiquette, and advice on how to avoid common tourist scams. With this comprehensive resource, you'll be well-prepared for any situation that may arise during your trip.

Culinary Delights: Mexican cuisine is renowned worldwide for its bold flavors, fresh ingredients, and rich traditions. This guide takes you on a culinary journey through Mexico, from the bustling food markets of Puebla to the gourmet restaurants of Mexico City. You'll discover regional specialties, street food favorites, and tips on where to find the best tacos, tamales, and mole. Recipes and cooking tips are also included for those who wish to bring a taste of Mexico back home.

Culture and Heritage: Mexico's cultural heritage is a vibrant tapestry woven from indigenous traditions, colonial influences, and contemporary innovations. This guide delves into the rich history and cultural practices that define Mexico, including festivals, music, dance, and art. You'll learn about the significance of Day of the Dead, explore the works of iconic artists like Frida Kahlo and Diego Rivera, and discover the vibrant world of Mexican folk art and crafts.

Outdoor Activities and Adventures: Mexico's diverse landscapes offer endless opportunities for outdoor enthusiasts. Whether you're an adrenaline junkie or a nature lover, this guide covers a wide range of activities, including hiking, surfing, diving, and bird watching. Detailed information on national parks, nature reserves, and adventure tours will help you plan your outdoor excursions, ensuring you experience the natural beauty and thrill of Mexico's great outdoors.

Shopping: Shopping in Mexico is a delightful experience, offering everything from traditional handicrafts to high-end fashion. This guide provides insights into the best shopping destinations, including local markets, artisan shops, and modern malls. You'll find tips on bargaining, recommendations for unique souvenirs, and information on where to find the finest silver jewelry, textiles, and pottery.

Day Trips and Excursions: While Mexico's cities are brimming with attractions, the surrounding regions offer equally captivating experiences. This guide suggests the best day trips and excursions from major cities, such as visiting the ancient ruins of Tulum from Playa del Carmen or exploring the picturesque town of Tequila from Guadalajara. Each excursion includes travel tips, highlights, and recommendations to make your day trip an enriching experience.

Entertainment and Nightlife: Mexico's vibrant nightlife and entertainment scene offer something for everyone. From lively mariachi performances and traditional dance shows to trendy bars and nightclubs, this guide covers the best places to unwind and enjoy Mexico's vibrant culture after dark. You'll find recommendations for the top venues, tips on local drinks to try, and advice on experiencing Mexico's unique blend of traditional and contemporary entertainment.

1.4 Travel Tips for Mexico

Mexico City is a vibrant hub where history and modernity coexist in harmony. Begin your exploration in the historic center, a UNESCO World Heritage site that includes the grand Zócalo square, surrounded by significant landmarks like the Metropolitan Cathedral and the National Palace. The ancient ruins of Templo Mayor offer a glimpse into the grandeur of the Aztec civilization. Don't miss the chance to immerse yourself in the local culinary scene; savor street food like tacos al pastor from El Huequito or enjoy a fine dining experience at Pujol, renowned for its innovative Mexican cuisine.

Wandering Through the Wonders of Chichen Itza: The Yucatán Peninsula is home to the awe-inspiring Chichen Itza, a testament to the ingenuity of the Mayan civilization. This archaeological marvel, featuring the iconic pyramid of El Castillo, is a must-visit. Explore the impressive Temple of the Warriors and the Great Ball Court, and afterward, cool off in the nearby cenotes, natural sinkholes that offer a refreshing escape. Cenote Ik Kil, with its clear waters and lush surroundings, is an excellent choice for a post-exploration swim.

Relaxing on the Riviera Maya: The Riviera Maya, with its stunning coastline, is a paradise for beach lovers. Playa del Carmen offers a lively beach scene with white sands and crystal-clear waters. Enjoy a day of sunbathing, snorkeling, and exploring the town's vibrant nightlife along Quinta Avenida. For a more tranquil experience, head to Tulum, where ancient Mayan ruins overlook serene beaches. The Tulum Ruins provide a dramatic backdrop to the turquoise sea, making it a perfect spot for relaxation and reflection.

Immersing in the Culture of Oaxaca: Oaxaca is a city rich in cultural heritage and artistic expression. Wander through the bustling Mercado Benito Juárez to discover traditional crafts and local delicacies. Oaxaca is particularly famous for its mole, a complex and flavorful sauce; try the seven varieties at La Olla or El Tule. The city also boasts nearby archaeological sites like Monte Albán, an ancient city that offers fascinating insights into early Mesoamerican civilization. Oaxaca's vibrant arts scene and culinary delights make it a cultural gem worth exploring.

Experiencing the Majesty of the Copper Canyon: In northern Chihuahua, the Copper Canyon presents a dramatic natural landscape, larger and deeper than the Grand Canyon. Experience the breathtaking views aboard the Chihuahua al Pacífico Railway, known as El Chepe, which traverses this stunning terrain.

CHAPTER 2
GETTING STARTED

2.1 Understanding Mexico

To truly understand Mexico, begin your journey in its vibrant capital, Mexico City. This sprawling metropolis is a living canvas where history and modern life collide in fascinating ways. Start at the Zócalo, the central square that is the heartbeat of the city. Here, the grand Metropolitan Cathedral and the National Palace stand as enduring symbols of the nation's past. The ancient ruins of Templo Mayor, located nearby, offer a glimpse into the Aztec civilization's sophisticated urban design and cultural richness. As you stroll through these historic streets, let the blend of old and new—evident in the colorful street art, bustling markets, and lively street performances—paint a vivid picture of Mexico's dynamic culture. This immersion into the city's essence will reveal how its storied past influences contemporary life.

Delving into Mayan Heritage at Chichen Itza: Traveling to Chichen Itza on the Yucatán Peninsula opens a window into the world of the ancient Maya. The grandeur of El Castillo, the pyramid that dominates the site, showcases the Maya's advanced understanding of astronomy and architecture. The site's alignment with astronomical events, such as the equinox, reflects the Maya's deep connection to the cosmos. Wander through the remnants of the Temple of the Warriors and the Great Ball Court, and you'll feel the weight of centuries of history. The experience is heightened by a visit to nearby cenotes like Cenote Ik Kil, where the natural beauty and serene atmosphere offer a moment of reflection on the Maya's relationship with their environment.

Immersing in Coastal Bliss at Playa del Carmen: To grasp Mexico's more relaxed side, head to Playa del Carmen along the Riviera Maya. This coastal town embodies the laid-back charm of Mexico's Caribbean coast. Relax on the pristine beaches where the gentle waves and soft sands invite you to unwind. Quinta Avenida, the main thoroughfare, pulses with life as you explore its array of shops, restaurants, and bars. The blend of vibrant nightlife and tranquil beachside moments offers insight into the Mexican approach to leisure and celebration. The contrasting experiences of sun-soaked relaxation and lively social scenes reveal the multifaceted nature of Mexican coastal life.

Savoring Oaxaca's Culinary and Cultural Richness: Oaxaca presents a deep dive into Mexico's cultural and culinary heritage. The city's markets, particularly Mercado Benito Juárez, burst with vibrant colors and aromatic scents, offering a feast for the senses. Oaxaca is renowned for its complex and flavorful moles, and tasting the seven varieties at establishments like La Olla provides an authentic culinary experience. The city's rich traditions are also evident in its art and festivals. Nearby Monte Albán, with its ancient ruins perched on a mountaintop, provides a historical backdrop that complements Oaxaca's lively cultural scene. Engaging with the local cuisine and traditions gives a tangible sense of the region's historical depth and cultural vibrancy.

Exploring the Majestic Copper Canyon: The Copper Canyon in northern Chihuahua offers a dramatic and awe-inspiring perspective on Mexico's natural beauty. The Chihuahua al Pacífico Railway, known as El Chepe, takes you on a remarkable journey through this vast and varied landscape. As the train winds through the canyon, you'll be treated to breathtaking views of rugged cliffs, lush valleys, and diverse wildlife. Stops like Creel provide opportunities to interact with the Tarahumara people, known for their incredible endurance and traditional way of life. This journey through the Copper Canyon reveals the grandeur of Mexico's natural landscapes and the resilience of its indigenous communities, offering a profound understanding of the country's diverse geography and cultures.

2.2 Geography and Climate

Mexico, a country of captivating contrasts and rich landscapes, stretches across the southern portion of North America. Its geography is as diverse as it is expansive, encompassing coastal plains, mountain ranges, arid deserts, and lush rainforests. To the north, it shares a border with the United States, while to the south, it is flanked by Guatemala and Belize. The country's vast terrain is interspersed with an intricate network of mountains, including the Sierra Madre Occidental and Sierra Madre Oriental, which run parallel to each other and extend from the northern to the southern borders. The rugged terrain of these mountain ranges is punctuated by the high altitudes of the Mexican Plateau, which forms a central core within the country. The Pacific Ocean graces Mexico's western coast, while the Gulf of Mexico and the Caribbean Sea border its eastern and southeastern shores. This geographic positioning endows Mexico with a variety of coastal environments, from the sandy beaches of Cancun and the Riviera Maya to the dramatic cliffs of Baja California. The country's diverse geography not only shapes its climate but also influences its myriad ecosystems, which range from desert landscapes in the north to tropical rainforests in the south.

Climate of Mexico

Tropical Climate: Mexico's tropical climate is prevalent along its coastal areas, including the Caribbean and Pacific coasts. In these regions, you can expect consistently high temperatures and high humidity throughout the year. Typically, temperatures range from 75°F (24°C) to 95°F (35°C). This climate features two distinct seasons: a hot and humid wet season from May to October, and a warm, drier period from November to April. The wet season is marked by frequent, brief showers or thunderstorms, while the dry season brings clear skies and lower humidity, ideal for beach outings and coastal adventures.

Arid and Semi-Arid Climate: The northern parts of Mexico, such as Sonora and Chihuahua, experience an arid and semi-arid climate. This region is known for its extreme temperature fluctuations. Summers can be intensely hot, with temperatures often soaring above 100°F (38°C), whereas winters can be considerably cooler. Rainfall is minimal, typically less than 10 inches (25 cm) per year, resulting in dry, desert-like conditions. Despite the scorching summer heat, the cooler winter months offer more comfortable conditions for travel and outdoor activities.

Temperate Climate: The central highlands of Mexico, including Mexico City and its environs, are characterized by a temperate climate. This area enjoys mild to cool temperatures year-round, with notable seasonal changes. From November to April, the dry season prevails, bringing clear skies and temperatures ranging from 50°F (10°C) to 75°F (24°C), which is ideal for sightseeing and exploring the city. The rainy season from May to October brings increased rainfall, which cools the temperatures and leads to occasional showers. This temperate climate provides a pleasant escape from the extreme heat found in lower altitudes.

Tropical Rainforest Climate: In the southernmost parts of Mexico, such as Chiapas and the Yucatan Peninsula, a tropical rainforest climate dominates. This climate is marked by consistently high temperatures and humidity, with abundant rainfall that supports lush, verdant landscapes. Temperatures in this region generally range from 70°F (21°C) to 90°F (32°C). The tropical rainforest climate has a pronounced wet season from May to October, featuring heavy rains, and a drier period from November to April. The lush environment and warm, wet conditions are perfect for exploring rich biodiversity and dense tropical forests.

Highland Climate: The highland regions of Mexico, including the Sierra Madre Occidental and Sierra Madre Oriental, experience a cooler climate compared to lower elevations. The highland climate is marked by cooler temperatures that drop with increasing altitude. These areas have a generally temperate climate with a clear dry season and a wet season that may include snowfall at the highest peaks. This climate is especially attractive for outdoor enthusiasts who enjoy hiking and exploring mountainous terrains.

Navigating Mexico's Geography and Climate: Travelers should consider Mexico's diverse geography when planning their visit. For a coastal retreat, aim for the dry season to maximize beach time and outdoor activities. If exploring the mountainous regions or historical cities, the cooler, dry months are ideal. It's also wise to check the local weather forecasts for specific regions before traveling, as conditions can vary significantly from one area to another. Understanding Mexico's climate patterns can greatly enhance your travel experience, ensuring that you are well-prepared for the weather and can fully enjoy the rich diversity of environments the country offers.

2.3 History and Culture

Mexico's history is an intricate dance of ancient civilizations and cultural confluences, a rich and vibrant narrative that has evolved over millennia. To truly understand Mexico, one must delve into its past, exploring the legacies of the Aztecs, Maya, and Olmecs—cultures that have shaped the country into the captivating destination it is today. The origins of Mexico's cultural heritage can be traced back to the early Mesoamerican civilizations, which laid the foundation for the nation's identity. Among these ancient cultures, the Olmecs are often regarded as the "mother culture" of Mesoamerica. Flourishing between 1200 and 400 BCE, the Olmecs established complex societies along the Gulf Coast, in what is now Veracruz and Tabasco. Their monumental stone heads and sophisticated art, found in places like La Venta and San Lorenzo, offer a glimpse into their profound understanding of astronomy and societal organization. The Olmecs were pivotal in shaping the region's cultural and technological advancements, setting the stage for the civilizations that followed. Following the Olmecs, the Maya civilization emerged in the Yucatán Peninsula around 250 CE. The Maya built an impressive array of cities, including Tikal, Uxmal, and Chichen Itza, each reflecting their remarkable achievements in architecture, mathematics, and astronomy. The Maya are renowned for their complex calendar systems and hieroglyphic writing, which continue to fascinate scholars and visitors alike. The ruins of these ancient cities offer a tangible connection to a time when the Maya excelled in creating a sophisticated culture deeply intertwined with the natural world.

As the Maya civilization waned, the Aztecs rose to prominence in central Mexico, centered around their capital, Tenochtitlán, now Mexico City. The Aztecs, who flourished from the 14th to the early 16th century, created a vast empire through a combination of military prowess, strategic alliances, and tribute systems. Their legacy is evident in the remnants of their grand temples and the intricacies of their social and religious practices. The Temple Mayor, located in the heart of modern-day Mexico City, stands as a testament to the grandeur of Aztec civilization and its complex pantheon of gods. The arrival of Spanish explorers in the early 16th century marked a profound turning point in Mexico's history. Hernán Cortés and his conquistadors encountered a world rich with cultural traditions and complex societies. The ensuing colonial period saw the blending of indigenous and Spanish influences, resulting in a unique mestizo culture that incorporates elements from both traditions. This fusion is visible in the vibrant festivals, traditional music, and colorful arts that define Mexican culture today.

Modern Mexico is a tapestry woven from this deep historical background. The country's cultural landscape is a dynamic mix of ancient traditions and contemporary expressions. From the bustling markets of Mexico City to the serene beaches of the Riviera Maya, Mexico offers a wealth of experiences that reflect its rich history and diverse cultural heritage. Visitors to Mexico are invited to walk through its storied past, explore its historic ruins, and immerse themselves in the vibrant traditions that continue to shape its identity. The journey through Mexico is not merely a passage through a country but an exploration of a civilization that has profoundly influenced the world.

2.4 Language and Communication

When visiting Mexico, it's essential to have a grasp of the local language to fully immerse yourself in the vibrant culture and communicate effectively with the locals. The official language of Mexico is Spanish, spoken by the vast majority of the population. While English is understood in tourist-heavy areas, especially in cities and popular destinations, having some knowledge of Spanish can significantly enhance your travel experience. It allows you to navigate more comfortably, engage in meaningful interactions, and show respect for the local customs and traditions.

Navigating Communication: Communication in Mexico goes beyond just speaking the language. It's also about understanding the cultural nuances and non-verbal cues that play a crucial role in everyday interactions. Mexicans are known for their warmth and friendliness, and they appreciate politeness and courtesy. A simple smile and greeting can go a long way in establishing rapport. When meeting someone for the first time, a handshake is common, and among friends and family, a hug or a kiss on the cheek is customary. Mexicans often use body language and gestures to convey messages. For instance, a thumbs-up is a positive gesture, indicating approval or agreement. On the other hand, pointing directly at someone can be considered rude, so it's better to use your whole hand to gesture. Understanding these subtleties can help you communicate more effectively and avoid misunderstandings.

Engaging with Locals: Engaging with locals can significantly enrich your travel experience in Mexico. Mexicans are generally very hospitable and enjoy sharing their culture with visitors. Showing an interest in their language and customs can open doors to memorable experiences and friendships. When invited to a Mexican home, it's polite to bring a small gift, such as flowers or sweets, as a token of appreciation. Participating in local traditions and festivities is another excellent way to connect with the culture. Mexico is known for its vibrant celebrations, such as Dia de los Muertos (Day of the Dead) and various regional festivals. Engaging in these events with a few Spanish phrases up your sleeve can enhance your understanding and enjoyment of the cultural richness.

2.5 Basic Spanish Phrases

Having a few key Spanish phrases in your repertoire can be incredibly helpful during your visit to Mexico. Start with basic greetings and expressions of politeness, as these are often the foundation of daily interactions. Saying "Hola" (Hello) and "Buenos días" (Good morning) or "Buenas tardes" (Good afternoon) are great ways to begin any conversation. Expressing gratitude with "Gracias" (Thank you) and responding with "De nada" (You're welcome) shows respect and appreciation. When asking for assistance, phrases like "Por favor" (Please) and "¿Puede ayudarme?" (Can you help me?) are useful. If you need directions, you might say, "¿Dónde está...?" (Where is...?). For example, "¿Dónde está el baño?" (Where is the bathroom?) or "¿Dónde está la estación de autobuses?" (Where is the bus station?). If you're trying to order food, "Quisiera..." (I would like...) followed by the name of the dish can be helpful.

Handling Emergencies and Seeking Help: In case of emergencies, knowing how to seek help in Spanish is crucial. If you need medical assistance, you can say, "Necesito un médico" (I need a doctor) or "Llamen una ambulancia" (Call an ambulance). For police assistance, "Llamen a la policía" (Call the police) is the phrase to use. It's also helpful to know how to ask for directions to the nearest hospital or police station: "¿Dónde está el hospital más cercano?" (Where is the nearest hospital?) or "¿Dónde está la estación de policía más cercana?" (Where is the nearest police station?).

2.6 Currency and Money Matters

When planning a trip to Mexico, understanding the local currency is essential. The official currency of Mexico is the Mexican Peso (MXN), often symbolized as $ or Mex$. One peso is subdivided into 100 centavos. Banknotes are available in denominations of 20, 50, 100, 200, 500, and 1,000 pesos, while coins come in 1, 2, 5, 10, and 20 pesos. Familiarizing yourself with the appearance of the currency can help avoid confusion and ease transactions during your stay.

Currency Exchange and Bureau de Change Locations

Currency exchange services are widely available throughout Mexico, particularly in major cities and tourist destinations. It's advisable to exchange some money before arriving, but for better rates, exchange bureaus, known as "Casa de Cambio," are a good option once in the country. These can be found in airports, shopping malls, and city centers. For example, in Mexico City, reliable options include Centro Cambiario Intercam at Avenida Paseo de la Reforma 255, Centro Histórico, and Globo Cambio at Terminal 1 of the Mexico City International Airport. Always compare rates and be mindful of service fees that might apply.

Using ATMs and Credit Cards:

ATMs are ubiquitous in Mexico and offer a convenient way to withdraw pesos using your debit or credit card. Ensure your card has international access, and inform your bank of your travel plans to avoid any service disruptions. Popular banks with extensive ATM networks include BBVA Bancomer, Santander, Citibanamex, Scotiabank, and HSBC. When using ATMs, opt for those attached to bank branches to minimize the risk of skimming devices and other fraudulent activities.

An Overview of Major Banks in Mexico

BBVA Bancome:

This is one of the largest banks in Mexico, offering extensive services for visitors. Their branches and ATMs are widespread, providing easy access to cash withdrawals, currency exchange, and financial advice. A notable branch for tourists is located at Paseo de la Reforma 390, Juárez, Mexico City.

Santander:

Provision of robust banking services, including efficient ATM networks and branches in key locations. They offer specialized services for international visitors, including assistance with currency exchange and traveler's checks. One of their convenient branches can be found at Avenida Insurgentes Sur 1602, Crédito Constructor, Mexico City.

Citibanamex:

Part of the global Citigroup, ensures a familiar banking experience for international travelers. They offer services such as global account access and currency exchange. Their branch at Avenida Paseo de la Reforma 510, Juárez, Mexico City, is a central location for tourists.

Scotiabank:

Serves both locals and visitors with a reliable network of ATMs and branches. They provide services tailored to international clients, including currency exchange and financial guidance. Visitors can find a branch at Avenida Insurgentes Sur 1458, Actipan, Mexico City.

HSBC:

This is another prominent bank with a strong presence in Mexico. They offer comprehensive services for travelers, including currency exchange and global account management. A notable branch is located at Avenida Paseo de la Reforma 347, Cuauhtémoc, Mexico City.

Budgeting for Your Trip:

Budgeting is crucial for a comfortable and enjoyable trip to Mexico. Costs can vary significantly depending on your destination and lifestyle. Major cities and tourist areas like Mexico City, Cancun, and Playa del Carmen tend to be more expensive. Budget travelers can expect to spend around $40-60 USD per day, covering basic accommodation, food, and transportation. Mid-range travelers might budget $100-150 USD per day, enjoying more comfortable accommodations and a wider range of activities and dining options. Luxury travelers should plan for $200-300 USD per day or more, depending on their preferences for high-end hotels, fine dining, and exclusive tours.

Tipping Etiquette:

Tipping is customary in Mexico and appreciated for good service. In restaurants, a tip of 10-15% of the bill is standard. Hotel staff, including bellboys and housekeeping, generally receive $1-2 USD per service. Taxi drivers do not usually expect tips, but rounding up the fare is common. For tour guides and other service providers, tipping is at your discretion based on the quality of service.

Managing Money Safely:

To manage money safely while traveling in Mexico, carry a combination of cash and cards. Avoid carrying large sums of cash, and use hotel safes for valuables. Be cautious when using ATMs, especially in less secure areas, and always cover your PIN. Regularly check your bank statements for any unauthorized transactions.

Digital Payment Options:

Digital payments are becoming increasingly popular in Mexico. Mobile payment apps like Mercado Pago, PayPal, and others are widely accepted in urban areas and among younger merchants. Ensure you have a backup payment method as not all places, especially in rural areas, accept digital payments.

CHAPTER 3
PLANNING YOUR TRIP

3.1 Best Time to Visit Mexico

Mexico is a vast country with diverse climates and regions, making it a year-round destination with something to offer every traveler. Its geographical diversity spans tropical beaches, arid deserts, lush jungles, and mountainous terrains, each with its own seasonal charm. Understanding Mexico's climate variations is key to planning the perfect trip, ensuring that visitors can make the most of their experience whether they are seeking sunny beach days, cultural festivals, or exploring ancient ruins.

Spring: Spring, from March to May, is one of the most popular times to visit Mexico. During these months, the weather is generally warm and pleasant across the country. In Mexico City and the central highlands, temperatures range from 15°C (59°F) to 25°C (77°F), making it an ideal time to explore the historic sites, museums, and vibrant neighborhoods. The coastal regions, including Cancun, Playa del Carmen, and Los Cabos, enjoy warm temperatures perfect for beach activities without the intense heat of summer. Spring is also the season of vibrant cultural events. Semana Santa (Holy Week) is celebrated with processions, festivals, and traditional ceremonies throughout the country. Additionally, the Festival Internacional Cervantino in Guanajuato, which takes place in April, offers a rich cultural experience with music, theater, and dance performances from around the world.

Summer: Summer in Mexico, from June to August, brings a mix of weather patterns depending on the region. The coastal areas experience high temperatures and increased humidity, with occasional afternoon showers that provide a refreshing break from the heat. This is the perfect season for those who love water activities such as snorkeling, scuba diving, and surfing. The Caribbean coast, including destinations like Cancun and the Riviera Maya, is particularly appealing during this time due to the warm waters and abundant marine life. Inland, the central highlands and northern regions offer a cooler and more temperate climate. Cities like San Miguel de Allende, Guadalajara, and Puebla provide a welcome respite from the coastal heat, with temperatures ranging from 20°C (68°F) to 30°C (86°F). These areas are ideal for exploring colonial architecture, artisan markets, and enjoying the local cuisine.

Autumn: Autumn, from September to November, is another excellent time to visit Mexico. The weather begins to cool down, and the rainy season tapers off, leaving the landscape lush and green. This season is characterized by numerous festivals, including the famous Dia de los Muertos (Day of the Dead) in late October and early November. This unique celebration, particularly prominent in Oaxaca and Mexico City, honors deceased loved ones with colorful altars, parades, and traditional foods. The Yucatan Peninsula, with its cenotes and Mayan ruins, is particularly appealing in autumn. The temperatures are more moderate, and the reduced humidity makes it comfortable to explore archaeological sites such as Chichen Itza and Tulum. Additionally, the Pacific coast, including Puerto Vallarta and Mazatlan, offers pleasant weather and fewer crowds compared to the peak tourist season.

Winter: Winter, from December to February, is the high season for tourism in Mexico. This period attracts visitors looking to escape the cold weather of the northern hemisphere. The coastal regions, particularly the Riviera Maya, Cancun, and Baja California, enjoy warm and sunny conditions, making it the perfect time for beach vacations. Temperatures in these areas range from 25°C (77°F) to 30°C (86°F), providing ideal conditions for swimming, sunbathing, and exploring coral reefs. Inland cities such as Mexico City, Oaxaca, and Merida also offer mild and pleasant weather during the winter months. This is an excellent time to explore cultural attractions, attend local festivals, and enjoy the festive atmosphere leading up to Christmas and New Year celebrations.

Additionally, the Monarch Butterfly Biosphere Reserve in Michoacan is a must-visit during winter, where millions of monarch butterflies migrate, creating a breathtaking natural spectacle.

Regional Variations and Special Considerations: While the general seasons provide a good framework for planning a trip to Mexico, it's important to consider regional variations. For instance, the Baja California Peninsula has a unique desert climate with mild winters and hot summers, making it an ideal destination for winter sun seekers. Conversely, the southern state of Chiapas experiences a tropical climate with a distinct rainy season from May to October, which is crucial for visitors planning to explore its lush rainforests and waterfalls. Travelers should also be aware of the hurricane season, which typically runs from June to November. While hurricanes are infrequent, it's advisable to monitor weather updates and consider travel insurance during these months, particularly when visiting the Caribbean coast and Gulf of Mexico.

3.2 Visa and Entry Requirements

Embarking on a journey to Mexico offers the promise of vibrant culture, stunning landscapes, and rich history. To ensure a smooth entry into this enchanting country, it is crucial to understand the visa requirements and entry procedures. Whether arriving by air, train, or road, being well-informed about the necessary documentation and protocols will enhance your travel experience and allow you to focus on exploring Mexico's many wonders.

Air Travel to Mexico: For most international visitors, air travel is the primary means of entering Mexico. Upon arrival at any of Mexico's international airports, such as Mexico City International Airport (Aeropuerto Internacional Benito Juárez), Cancun International Airport, or Los Cabos International Airport, travelers will encounter a straightforward entry process, provided they meet the visa requirements. Travelers from many countries, including the United States, Canada, and most European Union nations, do not require a visa for short visits. Instead, a tourist card, known as the Forma Migratoria Multiple (FMM), is necessary. This document is often distributed on the airplane or can be obtained at the airport upon arrival. It is essential to complete this form accurately, as it grants permission to stay in Mexico for up to 180 days. The FMM is usually issued free of charge, but it is important to retain it throughout your stay, as it will need to be presented upon departure.

Upon arrival, you'll proceed through immigration control where an officer will review your passport, FMM, and any supporting documents. Be prepared to answer questions about the purpose of your visit and your intended length of stay. In some cases, you might be asked to show proof of onward travel or sufficient funds for your stay. If you are traveling from a country with specific vaccination requirements, such as a yellow fever vaccination certificate, ensure these documents are readily accessible.

Entry via Train: Traveling to Mexico by train is less common but offers a unique and scenic way to enter the country. The most well-known route is the "Copper Canyon Train" or Chepe, which operates from Chihuahua to Los Mochis. However, for international travelers, trains often connect to major border cities like Ciudad Juárez or Tijuana. If you are entering Mexico by train from the United States, you will cross into Mexico via designated border stations. At these points, you will undergo customs and immigration checks. You will need to present your passport and, if required, the tourist card (FMM) that you obtained prior to or upon arrival. It is crucial to ensure that your travel documentation is in order before boarding the train to avoid any delays at the border. For train travelers entering from other countries, the process remains similar. Ensure that you check the specific requirements of your point of entry, as some stations may have additional procedures or documentation needs.

Road Travel: Driving into Mexico is a popular option for those seeking the freedom to explore at their own pace. Road travel from the United States is facilitated through several border crossings, including the San Ysidro-Tijuana border, Laredo-Nuevo Laredo, and El Paso-Ciudad Juárez. Each crossing has its own set of procedures. Before embarking on your road trip, ensure that your passport is valid for at least six months beyond your planned departure date from Mexico. If you're bringing a vehicle into Mexico, you'll need to obtain a Temporary Vehicle Importation Permit, which can be acquired online or at the border. This permit allows you to bring your vehicle into Mexico for up to 180 days. Along with your permit, you will need proof of ownership or rental agreement, and insurance coverage that is valid in Mexico. At the border, you'll present your passport, vehicle documents, and the FMM tourist card. Customs officials may conduct a vehicle inspection and ask questions about the purpose of your visit. It is advisable to have your travel itinerary and any relevant supporting documents readily available.

3.3 Health and Safety Tips

Maintaining health and safety during your visit to Mexico requires a blend of preparation, vigilance, and adaptability. By following recommended health precautions, ensuring food and water safety, and being mindful of your environment, you can enjoy a safe and healthy trip. With a proactive approach to health and safety, your experience in Mexico can be both rewarding and memorable.

Preparing for Health Concerns: Before embarking on a journey to Mexico, it is essential to prepare for potential health concerns that might arise. One of the primary considerations is ensuring that routine vaccinations are up to date. The Centers for Disease Control and Prevention (CDC) generally recommends vaccinations for hepatitis A and B, typhoid, and, depending on your travel plans, additional vaccines such as rabies. It's wise to consult with a healthcare provider well in advance of your trip to address these needs and discuss any other specific health precautions based on your destination within Mexico.

Drinking Water and Food Safety: One of the most common health issues faced by travelers in Mexico is gastrointestinal problems due to changes in diet and water. To minimize the risk of waterborne illnesses, it is advisable to drink bottled or purified water. Even when brushing your teeth or washing fruits and vegetables, it's prudent to use bottled water to avoid any potential contaminants. Additionally, avoid ice cubes made from tap water, as these may carry the same risks. Food safety is equally important. While Mexican cuisine is renowned for its delicious flavors, eating street food or from vendors with questionable hygiene practices can lead to foodborne illnesses. Opt for well-cooked meals and choose restaurants and food stalls that appear clean and have a high turnover of customers. When eating fresh produce, wash it thoroughly using clean water or peel it whenever possible.

Sun Protection and Hydration: Mexico's climate varies from arid desert conditions to tropical heat, which can have a significant impact on your health if not managed properly. Sun protection is crucial; applying a high-SPF sunscreen, wearing a wide-brimmed hat, and donning protective clothing can help shield your skin from harmful UV rays. Mexico's sunny weather can lead to dehydration, so it's important to drink plenty of fluids. Carry a water bottle and take regular sips, especially if you are engaging in physical activities or spending prolonged periods outdoors.

Insect-Borne Diseases: Insect-borne diseases, such as dengue fever, Zika virus, and malaria, are present in some regions of Mexico. To protect yourself, use insect repellent containing DEET, wear long-sleeved shirts, and long pants, and avoid areas with standing water where mosquitoes breed. Additionally, staying in accommodations with screened windows and air conditioning can further reduce your risk of mosquito bites.

Emergency Medical Services: Knowing how to access emergency medical services is a key aspect of ensuring safety during your visit. Major cities and tourist areas in Mexico have well-established healthcare facilities and pharmacies. In case of a medical emergency, the general emergency number is 911. It is beneficial to have a list of nearby hospitals and clinics, particularly if you are traveling to more remote areas. Hotels and tour operators can often provide recommendations and assistance in finding appropriate medical care if needed.

Travel Insurance: Travel insurance is a prudent investment for any international trip. It provides coverage for unexpected medical expenses, trip cancellations, and other emergencies that could disrupt your travel plans. Ensure that your policy covers medical evacuation and the specific risks associated with travel in Mexico. Carry a copy of your insurance details and keep it accessible during your trip.

Personal Safety Precautions: While Mexico is a vibrant and generally safe destination, it is important to exercise common sense and remain vigilant. Avoid displaying valuables and large amounts of cash, particularly in crowded areas. Use reputable transportation services and be cautious when exploring unfamiliar neighborhoods. It is advisable to travel in groups or with a guide, especially if venturing into less frequented areas.

Local Health Regulations: Be aware of local health regulations and recommendations that may impact your travel plans. For instance, certain areas may have specific health advisories or vaccination requirements. Stay informed about any updates or alerts from local authorities or international health organizations. Additionally, familiarize yourself with local customs and health practices to ensure that you respect and adhere to local norms.

Cultural Sensitivity and Health Practices: Understanding and respecting cultural practices related to health and hygiene is also important. Mexican culture may have different approaches to health and wellness, and being open to these differences can enrich your travel experience. Embrace local customs and practices, and seek local advice if you have any health-related concerns or questions.

3.4 Packing Essentials

Embarking on a trip to Mexico is a thrilling adventure, filled with vibrant cities, stunning landscapes, and a rich tapestry of culture. To ensure that your journey is as enjoyable and stress-free as possible, packing wisely is key. Understanding the essential items to bring, tailored to the diverse climates and activities you'll encounter, will help you make the most of your Mexican adventure.

Clothing Considerations: Mexico's climate varies significantly from region to region, so it's important to pack clothing suited to the specific areas you plan to visit. In coastal regions like Cancun and Playa del Carmen, where the weather is generally hot and humid, lightweight, breathable fabrics such as cotton and linen are essential. Pack comfortable shorts, sundresses, and flip-flops for daytime explorations. However, evenings may bring cooler temperatures, so include a light jacket or sweater to stay comfortable. In contrast, if your travels take you to higher altitudes such as Mexico City or the colonial highlands, temperatures can be cooler, particularly in the evenings. Layering is crucial in these regions; consider packing long-sleeve shirts, a medium-weight jacket, and versatile pants that can be adjusted according to the temperature. For visits to Mexico's mountainous regions or during the winter months, warmer clothing like sweaters, thermal layers, and sturdy hiking boots may be necessary.

Footwear for Every Terrain: Mexico offers a range of experiences, from beach lounging and city exploring to rugged hiking and archaeological site tours. Therefore, packing appropriate footwear is vital. Comfortable walking shoes or sneakers are indispensable for urban exploration, city tours, and casual outings. Opt for supportive footwear that can handle varied terrains if you plan on hiking or visiting natural reserves. For coastal destinations, water shoes or sandals are practical for beach activities and swimming. These protect your feet from sharp objects and provide comfort on sandy shores. If your itinerary includes visits to archaeological sites or uneven terrain, durable hiking boots with good ankle support will be beneficial. Additionally, packing a pair of dressy shoes or sandals for evenings out or formal occasions will ensure you're prepared for any event.

Essential Travel Documents and Health Items: When traveling to Mexico, carrying essential documents is crucial. Ensure that you have your passport, valid for at least six months beyond your intended stay, and any necessary visas or travel permits. For added security, make copies of these documents and store them separately from the originals. This precaution is useful in case of loss or theft. In terms of health and safety, pack a comprehensive travel medical kit. Include basic first-aid supplies such as band-aids, antiseptic wipes, and pain relievers. It's also wise to bring any personal medications you take regularly, along with a prescription for them. Mexico has an abundance of pharmacies, but having your medications on hand ensures you won't face any disruptions to your routine. Sun protection is a must for your Mexican travels. High-SPF sunscreen, broad-brimmed hats, and UV-protection sunglasses will shield you from the intense sun, especially in the higher altitudes and coastal areas. Don't forget insect repellent to guard against mosquitoes, particularly in tropical regions.

Technology and Electronics: To stay connected and capture memories of your Mexican adventure, packing the right technology is essential. Bring a smartphone with an international plan or local SIM card to ensure you have access to maps, translation apps, and emergency contacts. A portable charger is also a valuable addition, keeping your devices powered throughout long days of sightseeing. If you enjoy photography, pack a good quality camera to capture the stunning landscapes, vibrant city scenes, and historical sites. Extra batteries and memory cards will be useful for extended shooting sessions. Consider also packing a laptop or tablet if you plan on keeping a travel journal or need to manage work remotely during your trip.

3.5 Budgeting for Your Trip

Budgeting for a trip to Mexico involves understanding the various expenses you might encounter during your stay. Mexico offers a diverse range of experiences that can cater to different budgets, from luxurious resorts to budget-friendly hostels and street food. It is essential to plan according to your travel style and preferences to ensure a smooth and enjoyable experience.

Accommodation Costs: Accommodation is a significant component of travel expenses and varies widely depending on the location, type, and season. In bustling cities like Mexico City and tourist hotspots such as Cancun or Playa del Carmen, you will find a broad spectrum of lodging options. Luxury hotels and resorts in these areas can cost anywhere from $150 to $500 USD per night, offering high-end amenities and services. For those seeking mid-range accommodations, prices typically range from $50 to $150 USD per night, including comfortable hotels and boutique guesthouses. Budget travelers can find hostels and budget hotels with rates starting as low as $20 to $50 USD per night. In smaller towns and less tourist-centric areas, accommodation prices are often more affordable, providing good value for money.

Dining Expenses: Dining costs in Mexico can be highly variable depending on where you choose to eat. Street food and local eateries offer an authentic taste of Mexican cuisine at very reasonable prices, often between $5 to $15 USD per meal. These options not only provide an opportunity to sample delicious and diverse foods but also help keep your budget in check. Dining at mid-range restaurants, which offer a more extensive menu and a sit-down experience, typically costs between $15 to $30 USD per person. High-end restaurants and international cuisine establishments, particularly in major cities and tourist areas, can range from $40 to $100 USD or more per meal. To manage dining expenses effectively, consider exploring local markets and cooking some of your own meals if your accommodation allows.

Transportation Costs: Transportation is another critical aspect of budgeting for your trip. Mexico has a well-developed transportation network, including buses, taxis, and rideshare services. In major cities, public transportation such as metro and bus services is quite economical, often costing less than $1 USD per ride. Long-distance travel, whether by bus or domestic flights, should also be considered. Long-distance buses can range from $20 to $100 USD depending on the distance and comfort level, while flights between major cities can vary from $50 to $150 USD. In tourist areas, you may also use rideshare apps like Uber, which offer convenient transportation at competitive rates compared to traditional taxis. For those renting a car, prices typically start around $30 to $60 USD per day, not including fuel and insurance.

Attractions and Activities: The cost of attractions and activities in Mexico can vary greatly depending on what you choose to do. Entrance fees for popular tourist sites, such as ancient ruins, museums, and natural parks, generally range from $5 to $20 USD. Guided tours, which can enhance your experience and provide in-depth knowledge of the sites, often cost between $30 to $100 USD per person. Outdoor activities, such as snorkeling, diving, or adventure tours, can be more expensive, with prices ranging from $50 to $150 USD depending on the complexity and duration of the activity. It's a good idea to research and budget for specific attractions you want to visit, as well as any potential extra costs such as equipment rentals or transportation to the sites.

Currency Exchange and Fees: Managing your budget also involves understanding currency exchange and any associated fees. The Mexican Peso (MXN) is the local currency, and it is advisable to exchange some money before arriving in Mexico. Once there, you can exchange additional currency at local banks or exchange bureaus. Be aware of exchange rates and service fees, which can affect the amount of money you receive. Many establishments accept credit and debit cards, but it's still useful to carry some cash for smaller transactions and in areas where card payments are not accepted.

Budgeting for Miscellaneous Expenses: In addition to the main categories of expenses, consider budgeting for miscellaneous costs such as souvenirs, tips, and unexpected expenses. Souvenirs and gifts can range widely in price, so allocate a portion of your budget for these items based on your interests and shopping preferences. Tipping is customary in Mexico, with standard tips ranging from 10% to 15% in restaurants and small amounts for hotel staff, taxi drivers, and tour guides. Lastly, setting aside a contingency fund for unexpected expenses, such as medical emergencies or changes in travel plans, can provide peace of mind and prevent financial stress during your trip.

3.6 Accommodation Options

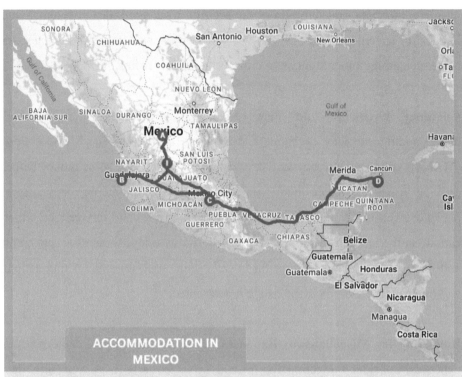

ACCOMMODATION IN MEXICO

Directions from México to Villa Las Palmas, Aguascalientes, Mexico

A	D	G
México	Sense, A Rosewood Spa, Carretera Federal Cancún SM Km. 298, Playa del Carmen, Quintana Roo, Mexico	Playa del Carmen, Mexico
B	**E**	**H**
Four Seasons Resort Punta Mita, Punta Mita, Nayarit, Mexico	Banyan Tree Mayakoba, Playa del Carmen, Quintana Roo, Mexico	Hotel Santa María, Manuel Carpio, Santa María la Ribera, Mexico City, CDMX, Mexico
C	**F**	**I**
The St. Regis Mexico City, Avenida Paseo de la Reforma, Colonia Cuauhtémoc, Mexico City, CDMX, Mexico	Hostel Mundo Joven Catedral, República de Guatemala, Historic center of Mexico City, Centro, Mexico City, CDMX, Mexico	Villa Las Palmas, Aguascalientes, Mexico

Mexico, a land of vibrant culture, stunning landscapes, and rich history, offers an array of accommodation options to suit every type of traveler. From opulent luxury hotels to charming vacation homes and unique stays, the country caters to all tastes and budgets. This comprehensive guide will delve into a selection of varied accommodations, each offering its own unique experience, ensuring that visitors can find the perfect place to rest, rejuvenate, and immerse themselves in the magic of Mexico.

The Four Seasons Resort Punta Mita

For those seeking unparalleled luxury and indulgence, Mexico boasts a selection of high-end hotels that promise an exquisite stay. The Four Seasons Resort Punta Mita, on the pristine beaches of the Riviera Nayarit, is renowned for its sophisticated elegance and impeccable service. This resort offers spacious villas with private pools, a world-class spa, and gourmet dining options. Prices for a stay at this resort start around $700 per night, with fine dining options available at various price points. More information and reservations can be found on their official website (https://www.fourseasons.com/puntamita).

St. Regis Mexico City: In the heart of Mexico City, the St. Regis Mexico City stands out for its blend of modern luxury and traditional charm. Overlooking the Chapultepec Park and the bustling Paseo de la Reforma, this hotel offers opulent rooms, a full-service spa, and personalized butler service. Rates begin at approximately $600 per night, with dining options ranging from casual to gourmet. For reservations and more details, visit their official website (https://shorturl.at/j3O8g).

The Rosewood Mayakoba: Located in Playa del Carmen, is a sanctuary of serenity and high-end comfort. Surrounded by lush mangroves and pristine beaches, this resort features luxurious suites, an exclusive spa, and multiple dining venues. Nightly rates start at about $800, with dining experiences reflecting the local and international cuisine. For bookings and further information, check their official website (https://shorturl.at/D2wK2).

Banyan Tree Mayakoba: Lastly, the Banyan Tree Mayakoba offers an unparalleled tropical experience with its private villas and picturesque surroundings. Situated in Playa del Carmen, this resort features an award-winning spa, a variety of dining options, and an emphasis on eco-friendly luxury. Prices start around $750 per night, with gourmet dining available at various price ranges. Visit their official website (https://www.banyantree.com/mexico/mayakoba) for more details.

Hostel Mundo Joven: Travelers on a budget need not sacrifice comfort or style while exploring Mexico. The Hostel Mundo Joven in Mexico City is a popular choice among budget-conscious travelers. Located near historic sites and bustling markets, it offers clean, affordable dormitories and private rooms starting at around $30 per night. The hostel also features a communal kitchen, free Wi-Fi, and a vibrant social atmosphere. More information is available on their official website (https://www.mundojovenhostels.com).

Playa del Carmen: In Playa del Carmen, the Budget Hostel Playa del Carmen offers a cozy and economical option. Located within walking distance of the beach and the vibrant Fifth Avenue, this hostel provides basic amenities with rates beginning at approximately $25 per night. Guests can enjoy a communal kitchen and relaxed atmosphere. Check out their official website (https://shorturl.at/anDb2) for further details.

Hotel Santa Maria: In Guadalajara is another excellent budget choice. This charming hotel combines affordability with comfort, offering rooms from around $50 per night. Situated in a central location, it provides easy access to the city's attractions, a friendly atmosphere, and basic amenities. Reservations and more information can be found on their official website (https://www.hotelsantamaria.com.mx).

Maya Hostel: For those visiting Tulum, the Maya Hostel offers budget-friendly accommodations with a unique touch. Starting at about $40 per night, it features dormitory-style rooms and private options, with access to a communal kitchen and relaxed common areas. Visit their official website (https://www.mayahosteltulum.com) for bookings and details.

Villa Las Palmas: For a more home-like experience, vacation rentals are a popular choice in Mexico. The Villa Las Palmas in Puerto Vallarta offers a luxurious yet homey atmosphere with its spacious five-bedroom property, private pool, and stunning ocean views. Prices start around $1,000 per night, with the option to customize meal plans and services. For more details, visit their official website (https://www.villalaspalmaspv.com).

Casa Palma: In Tulum, the Casa Palma is a beautifully designed vacation home with a focus on tranquility and elegance. This three-bedroom villa features a private pool, modern amenities, and a stylish design, with rates starting at approximately $800 per night. More information can be found on their official website (https://www.casapalmatulum.com).

The Hacienda de la Luz: in San Miguel de Allende offers a charming colonial-style home with lush gardens and a private courtyard. This four-bedroom rental is ideal for groups or families, with rates beginning around $700 per night. For reservations and details, visit their official website (https://www.haciendadelaluz.com).

Riviera Maya: Finally, in the Riviera Maya, the Casa Caracol provides an idyllic setting with its beachfront location and private amenities. This five-bedroom house offers stunning sea views, a private pool, and direct beach access, with prices starting at around $1,200 per night. For more information, visit their official website (https://www.casacaracolrivieramaya.com).

Unique Stays: Mexico's accommodation scene also includes some truly unique stays. The El Santuario in Tepoztlán is a boutique hotel offering a fusion of traditional Mexican architecture and modern luxury. With its beautiful gardens, spa, and wellness programs, it's an ideal retreat starting at around $200 per night. Visit their official website (https://www.elsantuariotepoztlan.com) for more information.

Downtown Mexico Hotel: In the heart of Mexico City, the Downtown Mexico Hotel combines historical charm with contemporary design. Set in a renovated 17th-century building, it offers unique rooms, a rooftop terrace, and an on-site restaurant. Rates start at approximately $150 per night. For reservations, visit their official website (https://www.downtownmexico.com).

The Hotel Xcaret Arte: In Playa del Carmen is a unique all-inclusive resort that blends luxury with cultural experiences. It features a stunning design, diverse dining options, and access to the nearby Xcaret parks. Prices begin around $500 per night, with inclusive dining and entertainment. Check their official website (https://www.hotelxcarete.com) for bookings.

Casa de la Playa: Lastly, the Casa de la Playa in Playa del Carmen offers an extraordinary luxury experience with its exclusive beachfront location, elegant suites, and personalized service. With rates starting at around $1,000 per night, it provides a secluded and opulent escape. For more information and reservations, visit their official website (https://www.casadelaplaya.com).

3.6 Getting to Mexico

Embarking on a journey to Mexico, a country rich in cultural heritage, stunning landscapes, and vibrant cities, requires thoughtful planning to ensure a smooth arrival. Whether you're flying into one of Mexico's bustling airports, traveling by train, or making the journey by road, each mode of transportation offers its own set of experiences and conveniences. Here's a detailed guide to help you navigate your way to Mexico, providing you with essential information on air travel, train options, and road travel.

Air Travel: Flying into Mexico is the most common and efficient way to start your adventure. Mexico boasts several international airports in major cities such as Mexico City, Cancún, Guadalajara, and Monterrey, each serving as a gateway to various regions of the country. Major airlines operate flights to Mexico from around the globe, offering a range of options to suit different budgets and preferences. For travelers coming from the United States, airlines like American Airlines, Delta Air Lines, and United Airlines provide numerous direct flights to Mexico's key airports. American Airlines, for instance, offers flights from cities such as New York, Dallas, and Los Angeles to destinations like Cancún and Mexico City. Ticket prices typically range from $250 to $600 for a round-trip, depending on the season and booking time. Delta Air Lines and United Airlines also offer competitive rates and multiple flight options, with similar price ranges. Booking these flights can be done through their respective websites: American Airlines (https://www.aa.com), Delta Air Lines (https://www.delta.com), and United Airlines (https://www.united.com).

For those traveling from Europe, airlines like British Airways, Air France, and Lufthansa provide excellent connectivity to Mexico. British Airways offers direct flights from London to Mexico City, with ticket prices starting around €600 for a round-trip. Air France connects Paris to Cancún and Mexico City, with prices generally around €650 to €700. Lufthansa provides flights from

Frankfurt and Munich, with similar pricing structures. Booking is available on their official websites: British Airways (https://www.britishairways.com), Air France (https://www.airfrance.com), and Lufthansa (https://www.lufthansa.com).

From South America, carriers such as LATAM Airlines and Aeroméxico offer flights to Mexico. LATAM connects cities like São Paulo and Buenos Aires to Mexico City, with round-trip fares starting at approximately $400. Aeroméxico, which is the national carrier, provides numerous flights from major South American cities to various Mexican destinations. Prices and schedules can be checked and booked through their websites: LATAM Airlines (https://www.latam.com) and Aeroméxico (https://www.aeromexico.com). Booking flights can be accomplished through airline websites or third-party travel agencies like Expedia, Kayak, or Skyscanner, which often offer comparative pricing and special deals. It is advisable to book well in advance to secure the best rates and to keep an eye on seasonal promotions.

Train Travel: Although Mexico does not have an extensive high-speed rail network like some other countries, train travel remains a viable and scenic option for those looking to experience the country from a different perspective. The most notable train route is the Copper Canyon Railway, operated by Ferromex. This route offers an extraordinary journey through the Copper Canyon region, one of Mexico's most breathtaking landscapes. The Copper Canyon Railway, known locally as the Chepe Express, runs between Los Mochis and Creel, traversing a vast expanse of canyons, mountains, and desert. The journey is renowned for its stunning vistas and includes several stops at picturesque towns and villages. Ticket prices for the Chepe Express vary depending on the class and time of booking, with options ranging from around $100 to $300 for a one-way journey. Reservations can be made through the official Chepe Express website (https://www.chepe.mx). For those interested in exploring Mexico's historic railways, the Tren Maya is a notable project aimed at enhancing rail travel across the Yucatán Peninsula. While not yet operational, it promises to connect popular destinations such as Cancún, Tulum, and Mérida, offering a unique way to explore the region. Keep an eye on updates from the Tren Maya official site (https://www.trenmaya.gob.mx) for future travel opportunities.

Road Travel: Driving to Mexico or within the country offers the freedom to explore at your own pace and discover hidden gems beyond the typical tourist routes. For international travelers driving from the United States, entering Mexico by road is facilitated through several border crossings. Major entry points include the crossings at Laredo, McAllen, and El Paso in Texas, and San Diego in California. Once in Mexico, renting a car is a popular option for exploring various regions. Driving in Mexico requires some preparation. Ensure that you have a valid driver's license, proof of insurance, and understand local driving regulations. It's advisable to check your car insurance policy to confirm coverage in Mexico. Additionally, familiarize yourself with the roads, as some areas may have toll roads (known as "cuotas") that require additional fees. For those driving from within Mexico, the country's road network is well-developed, with major highways connecting cities and popular tourist destinations. The Mexican Federal Highway System, marked by "Carreteras Federales," is generally in good condition, though some remote areas may have less reliable infrastructure. Maps and GPS navigation systems are invaluable for navigating the extensive road network.

3.7 Transportation Options

Navigating Mexico's transportation options offers a range of possibilities to suit various preferences and needs. From efficient public transit systems to convenient taxis and ride-sharing services, travelers can find numerous ways to explore urban areas and beyond. For those who prefer cycling or driving, Mexico provides well-developed routes and a variety of car rental options. By understanding the available transportation choices and planning accordingly, visitors can enhance their travel experience and make the most of their time in this vibrant and diverse country.

Public Transportation System: Mexico's public transportation network is both extensive and varied, offering numerous options for getting around the country. Major cities and tourist destinations are served by a range of transportation modes, each catering to different needs and preferences. In urban areas, the public transit system includes buses, metro systems, and light rail, which provide affordable and convenient travel options. In rural areas and smaller towns, public transportation often consists of local buses and shared taxis. In cities like Mexico City, the metro system is one of the most efficient and cost-effective ways to travel. The network is extensive, covering a vast area with 12 lines, each designated by a color and number, making navigation relatively straightforward. Fares for the metro are very affordable, typically around 5 pesos (approximately $0.30 USD) per ride. For longer distances and travel to surrounding areas, the Metrobus system provides a bus rapid transit service with dedicated lanes, helping to avoid traffic congestion. Fares for the Metrobus also start at around 6 pesos (approximately $0.35 USD). More information on the metro and Metrobus systems can be found on the official Sistema de Transporte Colectivo (STC) website (https://www.metro.cdmx.gob.mx).

In other major cities, such as Guadalajara and Monterrey, there are similar metro and bus systems offering reliable public transport options. Guadalajara's Sistema de Tren Eléctrico Urbano (SITEUR) features a light rail system, while Monterrey's Metrorrey provides both metro and bus services. These systems are also designed to be user-friendly, with clear signage and affordable fares. For information on SITEUR, visit the SITEUR website (https://siteur.guadalajara.gob.mx), and for Metrorrey, check out the Metrorrey website (https://www.metrorrey.gob.mx).

Taxi Services and Ride-Sharing Options: Taxis in Mexico are widely available and offer a convenient means of transportation, particularly in urban areas and tourist hotspots. The taxi service is generally regulated by local authorities, ensuring a standard level of safety and service. Several reputable taxi companies operate across Mexico, including Taxi Melchor Múzquiz, Taxi Capital, and Taxi Libertad in Mexico City. These companies are known for their reliable service and adherence to local regulations. Taxi fares vary by city and are typically calculated based on distance traveled. In Mexico City, for example, taxi fares start at around 8 pesos (approximately $0.45 USD) and increase with distance. For more information about taxi services in Mexico City, visit the Taxi Melchor Múzquiz website (https://www.taximelchor.com.mx).

Ride-sharing services have become increasingly popular in Mexico, offering a modern alternative to traditional taxis. Companies like Uber, DiDi, and Cabify are prominent in major cities and provide app-based ride-hailing options. Uber, for instance, operates across many urban centers, including Mexico City, Guadalajara, and Monterrey, offering a range of vehicle options from budget-friendly to premium rides. Fares for ride-sharing services vary depending on the distance, time of day, and type of vehicle selected, but they generally offer competitive rates compared to traditional taxis. More details can be found on the Uber Mexico website (https://www.uber.com/mx/en/).

DiDi and Cabify also offer similar services, with competitive pricing and various vehicle options. DiDi is particularly noted for its affordability and frequent promotions, while Cabify is known for its focus on customer service and safety features. Using ride-sharing apps is generally straightforward; users can request a ride, track their vehicle in real-time, and pay through the app, which enhances convenience and transparency. Visit the DiDi Mexico website (https://www.didiglobal.com/mx) and the Cabify Mexico website (https://www.cabify.com/mx) for more information.

Biking and Cycling Routes: Biking is an increasingly popular way to explore Mexico's cities and natural landscapes. Many urban areas have developed dedicated bike lanes and bike-sharing programs, promoting cycling as a sustainable and enjoyable mode of transport. In Mexico City, the Ecobici program allows residents and visitors to rent bicycles from numerous stations across the city. The program offers both short-term and long-term rentals, with a nominal fee for usage. The official Ecobici website (https://ecobici.cdmx.gob.mx) provides detailed information on bike rental options and station locations. Other cities, such as Guadalajara and Monterrey, have also introduced bike-sharing schemes and bike lanes, making it easier for cyclists to navigate urban areas.

Car Rental Companies: Renting a car in Mexico provides the flexibility to explore the country at your own pace. Several reputable car rental companies operate throughout Mexico, offering a range of vehicles to suit different needs and budgets. Among the leading car rental companies are Hertz, Avis, Budget, Enterprise, and Sixt.

Hertz is a well-established international car rental company with numerous locations across Mexico, including major airports and city centers. Hertz offers a variety of vehicles, from economy cars to luxury models, with competitive pricing and a reliable service network. For more details, visit the Hertz Mexico website (https://www.hertz.com/rentacar/location/mexico).

Avis is another prominent option, known for its extensive selection of vehicles and convenient rental locations throughout Mexico. Avis provides a range of rental options and is known for its customer service. Visit the Avis Mexico website (https://www.avis.com.mx) for more information.

Budget, as the name suggests, provides affordable rental options without compromising on quality. With locations in major cities and tourist destinations, Budget is a popular choice for cost-conscious travelers. More details can be found on the Budget Mexico website (https://www.budget.com.mx).

Enterprise, known for its customer service, offers a wide range of vehicles and flexible rental options, including long-term rentals. The Enterprise Mexico website (https://www.enterprise.com.mx) provides information on their services and locations.

Sixt, a global car rental company, also operates in Mexico, providing a selection of premium vehicles and high-end services. For more information, visit the Sixt Mexico website (https://www.sixt.com.mx).

CHAPTER 4
EXPLORING MEXICO CITY

4.1 Overview of Mexico City

Mexico City is a sprawling metropolis that captures the heart and soul of the nation. With over 21 million inhabitants, it stands as a vibrant blend of history, culture, and modernity, offering an adventure that is as diverse as it is captivating. Walking through its streets, one can feel the pulse of a city that thrives on its rich heritage and dynamic present. Stepping into Mexico City is akin to embarking on a journey through time. The city is built on the ruins of Tenochtitlán, the ancient Aztec capital, and echoes of this grand civilization resonate throughout the city. The Templo Mayor, an archaeological site in the city's center, provides a fascinating glimpse into the Aztec past. Here, amidst the remnants of ancient temples and artifacts, one can almost hear the whispers of age-old rituals and the bustling life of a once-mighty empire.

4.2 Must-See Attractions

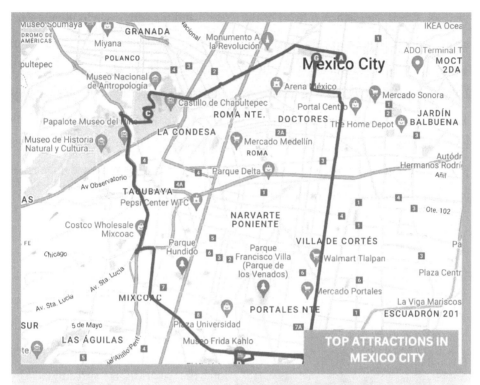

Directions from Mexico City, CDMX, Mexico to Mirador Torre Latino, Eje Central, Historic center of Mexico City, Centro, Mexico City, CDMX, Mexico

A
Mexico City, CDMX, Mexico

D
Frida Kahlo Museum, Londres, Del Carmen, Mexico City, CDMX, Mexico

B
Zócalo, Historic center of Mexico City, Centro, Mexico City, CDMX, Mexico

E
Frida Kahlo Museum, Londres, Del Carmen, Mexico City, CDMX, Mexico

C
Bosque de Chapultepec, Mexico City, CDMX, Mexico

F
Mirador Torre Latino, Eje Central, Historic center of Mexico City, Centro, Mexico City, CDMX, Mexico

Mexico City offers an array of must-see attractions that captivate and inspire visitors. From the historical heart of the Zócalo and the serene Chapultepec Park to the artistic legacy of the Frida Kahlo Museum and the ancient mysteries of Teotihuacan, each destination provides a unique and enriching experience. The Palace of Fine Arts adds a touch of cultural elegance to this diverse city. Together, these attractions create a mosaic of experiences that highlight the rich heritage and dynamic spirit of Mexico's capital. A visit to Mexico City is a journey through time and culture, offering unforgettable memories and a deeper appreciation of this remarkable metropolis.

- 4.2.1 Zócalo

Zócalo, or Plaza de la Constitución, is a historical and cultural epicenter that no visitor should miss. This expansive square, one of the largest in the world, is surrounded by architectural marvels that tell the tale of Mexico's rich past. The Zócalo is located in the Centro Histórico district and can be easily reached by Metro, with the Zócalo station opening directly onto the plaza. Visitors to the Zócalo will be awed by the imposing Metropolitan Cathedral, the largest cathedral in Latin America, and the National Palace, adorned with Diego Rivera's murals depicting Mexico's history. The square itself is often a stage for vibrant cultural events, protests, and celebrations, embodying the spirit of Mexico's capital. There is no entry fee to explore the Zócalo and its surrounding landmarks, making it an accessible attraction for all travelers. Walking through the Zócalo is like stepping into a living museum where the layers of history are palpable. From the ancient Templo Mayor ruins, remnants of the Aztec civilization, to the colonial and modern structures, every corner of the Zócalo tells a story. Visitors can take guided tours to delve deeper into the history and significance of this area or simply wander and soak in the atmosphere. The Zócalo's central location also makes it a perfect starting point for exploring the rest of Mexico City's Centro Histórico.

- 4.2.2 Chapultepec Park and Castle

Chapultepec Park, often referred to as the "lungs of Mexico City," is a vast green expanse that offers a refreshing escape from the urban hustle. Located in the Miguel Hidalgo borough, this park is easily accessible by Metro, with the Chapultepec station providing a convenient entry point. Spanning over 1,600 acres, it is one of the largest city parks in the Western Hemisphere and home to numerous attractions, including the Chapultepec Castle.

Perched atop a hill within the park, Chapultepec Castle is a historic gem with breathtaking views of the city. The castle, once an imperial residence, now houses the National Museum of History. The entry fee to the castle is around 80 MXN (approximately 4 USD), and it is free for children under 13, seniors, and students with a valid ID. The museum showcases Mexico's history through its extensive collection of artifacts, murals, and exhibits. Visitors to Chapultepec Park can enjoy a variety of activities, from boating on the park's lakes to visiting the renowned Chapultepec Zoo and the Museum of Modern Art. The park is an ideal spot for picnicking, jogging, or simply unwinding in nature. Chapultepec Park and Castle provide a perfect blend of history, culture, and recreation, making them a must-visit for anyone exploring Mexico City.

- 4.2.3 Frida Kahlo Museum

The Frida Kahlo Museum, known as La Casa Azul (The Blue House), is a vibrant tribute to one of Mexico's most iconic artists. Located in the charming Coyoacán neighborhood, this museum is dedicated to the life and work of Frida Kahlo. The museum is accessible by Metro, with the Coyoacán station being the closest. La Casa Azul is not just a museum; it is the home where Frida was born, lived, and died, making it an intimate glimpse into her life. The house itself, painted in a striking cobalt blue, is filled with Kahlo's personal belongings, artworks, and artifacts. The entry fee is 250 MXN (approximately 12.50 USD) for general admission and 45 MXN (approximately 2.25 USD) for Mexican citizens on Sundays. Tickets can be purchased online in advance to avoid long queues. Visitors to the Frida Kahlo Museum will find themselves immersed in the world of this remarkable artist. The museum's exhibits include her paintings, drawings, and sketches, as well as her distinctive clothing and medical equipment. The lush garden and courtyard of La Casa Azul offer a peaceful retreat where visitors can reflect on Kahlo's extraordinary life and legacy. The museum shop also provides an array of Frida-inspired merchandise, perfect for souvenirs.

- 4.2.4 Teotihuacan Pyramids

A short drive northeast of Mexico City lies the awe-inspiring Teotihuacan Pyramids, one of the most significant archaeological sites in the world. Known as the "City of the Gods," Teotihuacan was a thriving metropolis long before the Aztec civilization. Visitors can reach Teotihuacan by bus from Mexico City's Terminal del Norte, with a journey time of about an hour. The entrance fee to Teotihuacan is 80 MXN (approximately 4 USD), and the site is open daily. Once inside, visitors can explore the monumental Pyramids of the Sun and the Moon, the Temple of the Feathered Serpent, and the Avenue of the Dead. Climbing the pyramids offers a breathtaking panorama of the ancient city and the surrounding landscape, providing a sense of the grandeur of this ancient civilization. Teotihuacan's significance extends beyond its architectural marvels; it was a major cultural and religious center. Guided tours are available for those who wish to delve deeper into the history and mysteries of Teotihuacan. The site also features a museum that houses artifacts and provides context to the ancient city's history. A visit to Teotihuacan is a journey back in time, offering a profound connection to Mexico's pre-Hispanic heritage.

4.3 Hidden Gems of Mexico City

Mexico City, with its vast tapestry of history and culture, hides within its bustling streets and grand plazas a series of lesser-known treasures. These hidden gems, often overshadowed by the city's more prominent landmarks, offer a unique glimpse into the soul of Mexico's capital. Each location has its own story, waiting to be discovered by those willing to wander off the beaten path. Here are five such hidden gems that promise to enchant and captivate anyone seeking a deeper connection with this vibrant metropolis.

Xochimilco's Floating Gardens: While many visitors are familiar with Xochimilco's colorful trajineras (flat-bottomed boats), few delve into the full history of these floating gardens. Xochimilco, a UNESCO World Heritage site, was once a sprawling network of canals built by the Aztecs for agriculture. The chinampas, or floating gardens, are a testament to the ingenuity of pre-Hispanic engineering. These artificial islands, created from layers of mud and vegetation, allowed the Aztecs to cultivate crops year-round in the lake's rich soil. Today, a visit to Xochimilco offers more than just a boat ride. As you drift through the canals, you'll see the remnants of an ancient agricultural system that sustained a powerful empire. The experience is enhanced by the lively atmosphere of mariachi bands and the tantalizing aromas of traditional Mexican food being cooked on the boats. It's a living, breathing piece of history that continues to thrive amidst the urban sprawl of modern Mexico City.

San Ángel's Saturday Art Market: In the charming neighborhood of San Ángel, the Saturday Art Market, or "Mercado de Artesanías," is a hidden gem that bursts with local creativity. San Ángel, a historic district with cobblestone streets and colonial architecture, transforms into an open-air gallery every weekend. Here, artists and artisans display their handcrafted goods, ranging from vibrant paintings and intricate jewelry to colorful textiles and traditional pottery. The market's origins date back to the early 20th century, when local artists sought a space to showcase their work. Over time, it has grown into a cultural institution, drawing both locals and tourists who come to appreciate the rich tapestry of Mexican art and craft. Wandering through the stalls, you'll find more than just souvenirs; you'll encounter the passion and talent of Mexico's artistic community.

La Roma's Casa Lamm: In the heart of the Roma neighborhood, Casa Lamm stands as a testament to Mexico City's elegant past. Built in 1911 as the private residence of a wealthy family, this mansion has been transformed into a cultural center and art gallery. Its stunning architecture, characterized by ornate ironwork and exquisite mosaics, reflects the opulence of early 20th-century Mexico. Casa Lamm's transformation into a cultural hub began in the 1980s, when it was acquired by the Mexican philanthropist, José Lamm. The mansion now hosts art exhibitions, literary events, and concerts, providing a refined space for the city's creative minds.

Coyoacán's Frida Kahlo Museum: Often overshadowed by its more famous neighbor, the Museo Frida Kahlo, or "Casa Azul," is a hidden gem tucked away in the bohemian neighborhood of Coyoacán. This blue-hued house was the lifelong home of the iconic artist Frida Kahlo and her husband, Diego Rivera. The museum offers an intimate glimpse into Kahlo's world, with personal artifacts, vibrant paintings, and evocative photographs that capture her tumultuous yet passionate life. The origins of the museum trace back to 1958, when Kahlo's former residence was opened to the public. It was preserved with care by her husband Diego Rivera and remains a shrine to her legacy.

4.4 Exploring Mexico City's Neighborhoods

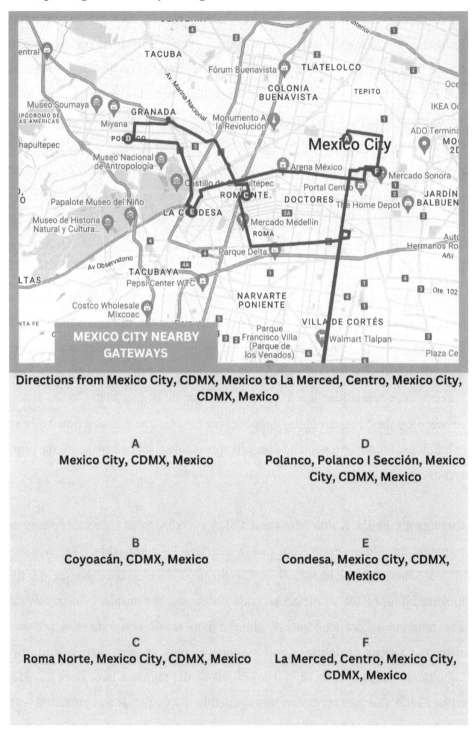

Directions from Mexico City, CDMX, Mexico to La Merced, Centro, Mexico City, CDMX, Mexico

A Mexico City, CDMX, Mexico	**D** Polanco, Polanco I Sección, Mexico City, CDMX, Mexico
B Coyoacán, CDMX, Mexico	**E** Condesa, Mexico City, CDMX, Mexico
C Roma Norte, Mexico City, CDMX, Mexico	**F** La Merced, Centro, Mexico City, CDMX, Mexico

Mexico City is a sprawling metropolis with a rich tapestry of neighborhoods, each offering its own unique flavor and character. From historical enclaves to trendy districts, exploring these neighborhoods reveals the city's multifaceted personality. Each area tells its own story, blending the past with the present and inviting visitors to experience the essence of Mexico City in all its vibrancy. Here's a guide to distinct neighborhoods that will captivate and inspire any traveler.

Coyoacán: Coyoacán, a neighborhood that feels like a charming village within the sprawling city, is a haven for those seeking a blend of history and bohemian flair. As you wander through its cobblestone streets, you'll encounter colorful murals, quaint cafes, and artisan shops that reflect its artistic spirit. Coyoacán is perhaps best known for being the home of Frida Kahlo and Diego Rivera, with Kahlo's former residence, Casa Azul, now a museum dedicated to her life and art. The area exudes a laid-back atmosphere, perfect for leisurely strolls through the central plaza, where locals gather to enjoy street performances and artisan markets. The historic charm of Coyoacán is further enhanced by its colonial architecture and the serene ambiance of the nearby Viveros de Coyoacán park. Visiting Coyoacán feels like stepping into a vibrant yet peaceful world, where the creative energy of its famous residents lingers in the air.

Roma: Roma, once a posh residential area, has evolved into one of Mexico City's most trendy and artistic neighborhoods. Known for its striking architecture, Roma features an eclectic mix of early 20th-century buildings and contemporary design. The area is a canvas for street art, with vibrant murals and graffiti that add a splash of color to its urban landscape. As you explore Roma, you'll discover a wealth of hip cafes, vintage shops, and boutique galleries. The neighborhood's culinary scene is equally impressive, with a variety of restaurants offering everything from gourmet tacos to artisanal pastries. Roma's atmosphere is youthful and dynamic, making it a favorite spot for those looking to experience the city's modern cultural pulse.

Polanco: Polanco stands as a symbol of Mexico City's contemporary luxury and sophistication. Often compared to New York's Upper East Side, Polanco is renowned for its high-end shopping, fine dining, and elegant residences. The area is home to luxury boutiques, international brands, and some of the city's most exclusive restaurants. One of Polanco's standout features is Avenida Presidente Masaryk, often referred to as Mexico City's "Champs-Élysées." Here, you'll find flagship stores of global fashion houses, alongside upscale dining establishments and art galleries. The neighborhood also boasts the beautiful Chapultepec Park, offering a green oasis where visitors can escape the urban hustle and enjoy leisurely walks or boat rides on the park's lakes.

Condesa: Condesa is a neighborhood that seamlessly blends old-world charm with modern vibrancy. Characterized by its tree-lined avenues and historic buildings, Condesa is a testament to Mexico City's ability to preserve its heritage while embracing contemporary life. The area is dotted with Art Deco architecture, giving it a distinctive and elegant appearance. The neighborhood's bustling nightlife and gastronomic scene are major draws. From lively bars and nightclubs to chic cafes and gourmet eateries, Condesa offers a diverse range of dining and entertainment options.

La Merced: For a taste of Mexico City's raw energy and vibrant market culture, La Merced is the place to visit. This bustling neighborhood is home to one of the city's largest and most famous markets, where an array of sights, sounds, and smells create an exhilarating sensory experience. La Merced Market is a labyrinth of stalls selling everything from fresh produce and meats to spices, herbs, and traditional Mexican sweets.

4.5 Dining and Nightlife in Mexico City

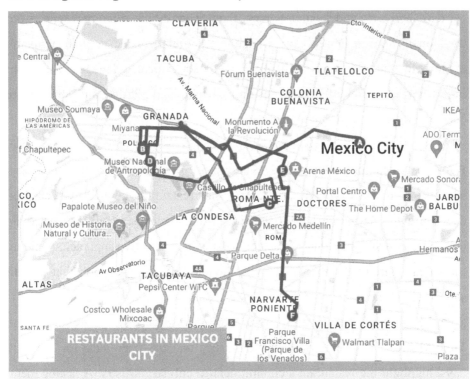

Directions from Mexico City, CDMX, Mexico to El Vilsito, Avenida Universidad, Narvarte Poniente, Mexico City, CDMX, Mexico

A
Mexico City, CDMX, Mexico

D
Maison Belén, Avenida Emilio Castelar, Polanco, Polanco IV Sección, Mexico City, CDMX, Mexico

B
Pujol, Tennyson, Polanco, Polanco IV Sección, Mexico City, CDMX, Mexico

E
Hanky Panky Cocktail Bar, Turín, Juárez, Mexico City, CDMX, Mexico

C
Licorería Limantour, Avenida Álvaro Obregón, Roma Norte, Mexico City, CDMX, Mexico

F
El Vilsito, Avenida Universidad, Narvarte Poniente, Mexico City, CDMX, Mexico

Mexico City's vibrant dining and nightlife scene is a testament to its rich cultural heritage and contemporary flair. The city's offerings span from traditional Mexican fare to cutting-edge international cuisine, complemented by a nightlife that ranges from lively bars to sophisticated lounges. Here's an in-depth exploration of diverse locations where food, drink, and atmosphere converge to create unforgettable experiences.

Pujol: Situated in the upscale neighborhood of Polanco, Pujol stands as a beacon of culinary excellence. This renowned restaurant, helmed by acclaimed chef Enrique Olvera, offers a dining experience that elevates traditional Mexican cuisine to new heights. Pujol is celebrated for its innovative approach, blending traditional ingredients with modern techniques to create a menu that is both sophisticated and deeply rooted in Mexican culture. The tasting menu at Pujol is a journey through the diverse flavors of Mexico. Signature dishes such as the Mole Madre, a rich and complex mole sauce that has been aged for over 100 days, highlight the restaurant's commitment to culinary artistry. A tasting menu can range from $150 to $250 per person, depending on the selections and wine pairings. The restaurant is open for lunch from 1:00 PM to 3:30 PM and for dinner from 8:00 PM to 11:00 PM, with reservations highly recommended due to its popularity.

Licorería Limantour: In the heart of Roma, Licorería Limantour has established itself as a premier destination for cocktail enthusiasts. Known for its creative concoctions and stylish ambiance, this cocktail bar combines a sophisticated setting with innovative mixology. The bar is named after the historic Limantour building where it is located, adding a touch of heritage to its modern allure. The drink menu at Licorería Limantour is a testament to the art of cocktail creation. Signature drinks include the "Oaxaca Old-Fashioned," which infuses traditional Mexican mezcal with a modern twist, and the "Aviation," a gin-based cocktail with a refreshing citrus profile. Each drink is meticulously crafted using high-quality ingredients and unique flavor combinations. The atmosphere at Licorería Limantour is chic and inviting, with a sleek design that features dark wood, plush seating, and ambient lighting. Prices for cocktails range from $10 to $15, reflecting the premium ingredients and craftsmanship involved. The bar operates from 6:00 PM to 2:00 AM, making it an ideal spot for a night out.

Maison Belén: In the vibrant neighborhood of La Condesa, Maison Belén offers a unique blend of French and Mexican cuisine. This restaurant exudes a charming, rustic elegance, with its décor featuring vintage French elements and a cozy, intimate atmosphere. Maison Belén's menu reflects a fusion of French culinary techniques with traditional Mexican flavors, resulting in a dining experience that is both refined and accessible. The menu includes dishes such as "Duck Confit with Mole," which pairs the rich, savory flavors of French duck with a traditional Mexican mole sauce, and "Crêpes Suzette," a classic French dessert with a zesty orange sauce. The restaurant also boasts an impressive selection of wines, both local and international, to complement the diverse menu. Maison Belén offers a refined yet relaxed dining experience, with prices ranging from $20 to $50 per person, depending on the menu choices and wine selections. The restaurant is open for lunch from 1:00 PM to 4:00 PM and for dinner from 7:00 PM to 11:00 PM. The warm and inviting atmosphere makes it a perfect choice for a leisurely meal or a special occasion.

Hanky Panky: This speakeasy-style bar, accessed through a discreet entrance at a traditional Mexican restaurant, offers an exclusive and intimate setting for enjoying expertly crafted cocktails. The bar's retro ambiance, complete with vintage décor and dim lighting, evokes the glamour of the Prohibition era. The cocktail menu at Hanky Panky is a curated selection of classic and contemporary drinks. Highlights include the "Hanky Panky," a gin-based cocktail with a touch of vermouth and Fernet, and the "Negroni," a sophisticated blend of gin, Campari, and vermouth. Each cocktail is prepared with precision and flair by skilled mixologists. Hanky Panky is known for its exclusivity, with reservations required for entry. Cocktails are priced around $15 each, reflecting the high quality of the ingredients and the artistry involved in their creation. The bar operates from 8:00 PM to 2:00 AM, offering a sophisticated and secretive night out in the heart of Mexico City.

El Vilsito: The vibrant, bustling atmosphere of El Vilsito, with its open kitchen and lively crowds, captures the essence of traditional Mexican dining. The star of the menu is the tacos al pastor, which feature tender, marinated pork cooked on a vertical spit and served with fresh pineapple, cilantro, and onions. The tacos are simple yet incredibly flavorful, reflecting the time-honored techniques that have made El Vilsito a beloved institution. The taquería also offers a variety of other tacos, quesadillas, and salsas that showcase the depth of Mexican street food. El Vilsito is known for its affordability, with tacos priced around $1 to $2 each, making it an excellent option for a casual and delicious meal. The taquería is open from 6:00 PM to 3:00 AM, providing a perfect late-night dining option for those seeking an authentic taste of Mexico City.

CHAPTER 5
DISCOVERING THE YUCATÁN PENINSULA

5.1 Overview of the Yucatán Peninsula

Imagine stepping into a land where the past and present entwine in an unforgettable embrace. The Yucatán Peninsula, a captivating region in southeastern Mexico, is exactly that—a place where ancient history and breathtaking natural beauty come together to create an unparalleled travel experience. With its azure waters, lush jungles, and ancient ruins, this peninsula offers more than just a getaway; it provides a journey into the heart of a vibrant and storied culture. As you wander along the sunlit beaches of the Yucatán, you'll be enchanted by the pristine beauty that seems to stretch endlessly before you. Picture yourself sinking your toes into the powdery white sands of Tulum, a coastal paradise where the Caribbean Sea's crystal-clear waters invite you to dive in and explore. The gentle waves caress the shore, and the backdrop of ancient Mayan ruins creates a striking contrast that makes this beach not just a place to relax, but a destination that tells a story. Each sunset here is a masterpiece, painting the sky in shades of orange and pink, while the tranquil sea whispers secrets of the past.

Venturing beyond the beaches, the Yucatán Peninsula reveals a landscape teeming with natural wonders. The region is dotted with cenotes—natural sinkholes filled with fresh, cool water that offer a refreshing escape from the sun. These cenotes, formed over millennia, are not just beautiful; they are sacred sites for the Maya, who believed they were portals to the underworld. Swimming or diving in these ancient pools is akin to stepping back in time, experiencing a piece of the earth that has remained unchanged for centuries. The allure of the Yucatán extends deep into its jungles and ruins, where the echoes of the Maya civilization still resonate. The majestic ruins of Chichén Itzá stand as a testament to the architectural genius and astronomical knowledge of the Maya. The sheer scale of the Pyramid of Kukulcán and the intricacy of the Temple of the Warriors are awe-inspiring, each stone telling a story of a civilization that flourished long before our time. Walking among these ruins, you can't help but feel a profound connection to the past, as if the ghosts of the Maya are guiding you through their history.

Equally enchanting is the city of Mérida, a vibrant hub of culture and history that pulsates with life. Known for its colonial architecture, bustling markets, and lively festivals, Mérida offers a taste of authentic Yucatán culture. The city's streets are lined with colorful buildings, and the air is filled with the sounds of traditional music. Every corner of Mérida seems to invite exploration, from its charming cafes to its rich museums. The Yucatán Peninsula is more than just a destination; it is an invitation to experience a place where history, nature, and culture converge in a way that captivates the heart and mind. Whether you're lounging on a sun-drenched beach, exploring ancient ruins, or immersing yourself in local traditions, the Yucatán offers a journey that is as diverse as it is unforgettable.

5.2 Must-See Attractions

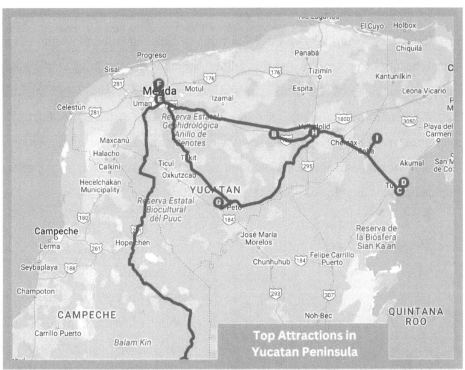

Top Attractions in Yucatan Peninsula

Directions from Yucatan Peninsula to Punta Laguna, Quintana Roo Nuevo Durango - Coba, Quintana Roo, Mexico

A Yucatan Peninsula	**D** Cenotes Casa Tortuga Tulum, Cancun - Tulum Highway, Ejidal, Tulum, Quintana Roo, Mexico	**G** Ek-Balam, Yucatan, Mexico
B Chichen-Itza, Yucatan, Mexico	**E** Merida, Yucatan, Mexico	**H** Valladolid, Yucatan, Mexico
C Tulum Archaeological Zone, Zona Hotelera Tulum, Tulum, Quintana Roo, Mexico	**F** Cenote Xlacah, Merida, Yucatan, Mexico	**I** Punta Laguna, Quintana Roo, Mexico

The Yucatán Peninsula is a region of immense natural beauty, rich history, and vibrant culture, offering a wealth of must-see attractions that captivate and inspire visitors. From the awe-inspiring ruins of Chichen Itza and Tulum to the serene beauty of its cenotes and the cultural vibrancy of Mérida and Valladolid, each destination provides a unique and enriching experience. Exploring the Yucatán Peninsula is a journey through time and nature, offering unforgettable memories and a deeper appreciation of Mexico's remarkable heritage. Whether you are seeking adventure, relaxation, or cultural immersion, the Yucatán Peninsula has something to offer every traveler.

- 5.2.1 Chichen Itza

Chichen Itza, one of the New Seven Wonders of the World, stands as a testament to the grandeur and sophistication of the ancient Maya civilization. Located in the northern part of the Yucatán Peninsula, this archaeological site is a must-visit for anyone interested in history, culture, and architecture. Chichen Itza is easily accessible by car or bus from major cities like Cancún, Playa del Carmen, and Mérida, with the journey taking approximately two to three hours. The entrance fee to Chichen Itza is around 533 MXN (approximately 27 USD) for international visitors, which includes a mandatory state fee. The site is open daily from 8 am to 5 pm. As you step into Chichen Itza, the first sight that captures your attention is the magnificent Pyramid of Kukulcán, also known as El Castillo. This pyramid, with its precise astronomical alignments, is a marvel of engineering and a focal point of the site. Exploring Chichen Itza offers more than just a glimpse of the iconic pyramid. The Temple of the Warriors, the Great Ball Court, and the observatory known as El Caracol are just a few of the numerous structures that reveal the advanced knowledge of the Maya in various fields, from astronomy to architecture.

- 5.2.2 Tulum Ruins

Perched on a cliff overlooking the turquoise waters of the Caribbean Sea, the Tulum Ruins offer a unique blend of natural beauty and historical intrigue. Located on the eastern coast of the Yucatán Peninsula, Tulum is about a 1.5-hour drive from Playa del Carmen and a 2-hour drive from Cancún. The site is also accessible by bus, with regular services from these major tourist hubs. The entrance fee to Tulum Ruins is 85 MXN (approximately 4 USD), and the site is open daily from 8 am to 5 pm. Tulum was one of the last cities built and inhabited by the Maya, and its coastal location provided strategic advantages for trade and defense. The most iconic structure at Tulum is El Castillo, a pyramid that served as a lighthouse guiding Maya traders navigating the coast. Walking through Tulum, visitors can explore the Temple of the Frescoes, which features intricate murals depicting various deities, and the Temple of the Descending God, dedicated to the mysterious diving figure. The site's location also offers spectacular views of the Caribbean, making it a perfect spot for photography and relaxation. After exploring the ruins, visitors can descend to the beach below and take a refreshing swim in the clear, warm waters.

- 5.2.3 Cenotes

The Yucatán Peninsula is renowned for its cenotes, natural sinkholes filled with crystal-clear freshwater, created by the collapse of limestone bedrock. These cenotes were sacred to the ancient Maya, who believed they were portals to the underworld. Today, they offer visitors a unique opportunity to swim, snorkel, and dive in pristine, otherworldly settings. There are thousands of cenotes scattered across the Yucatán Peninsula, with some of the most famous ones located near the cities of Tulum, Valladolid, and Mérida. Popular cenotes like Ik Kil, Dos Ojos, and Gran Cenote can be reached by car or organized tours, which often include transportation and equipment rental. Entry fees vary but typically range from 100 to 300 MXN (approximately 5 to 15 USD) depending on the cenote and the activities offered. Visiting a cenote is an unforgettable experience. The crystal-clear waters, often surrounded by lush vegetation and dramatic rock formations, create a tranquil and enchanting environment. Many cenotes have platforms for jumping and ladders for easy access to the water. For those interested in diving, the underwater caverns and tunnels provide a thrilling adventure. It's advisable to bring a swimsuit, water shoes, and a waterproof camera to fully enjoy and capture the beauty of these natural wonders.

- 5.2.4 Mérida

Mérida, the vibrant capital of the Yucatán state, is a city rich in colonial charm, cultural heritage, and modern amenities. Located in the northwest of the Yucatán Peninsula, Mérida is a gateway to exploring the region's historical sites, natural wonders, and vibrant local culture. The city is well-connected by air, with the Manuel Crescencio Rejón International Airport serving numerous domestic and international flights. It is also accessible by bus from major cities like Cancún and Playa del Carmen. Known as the "White City" due to its elegant white-stone buildings, Mérida offers a plethora of attractions and activities. The city's historic center is a treasure trove of colonial architecture, with landmarks such as the Mérida Cathedral, built in the 16th century, and the Palacio de Gobierno, featuring impressive murals depicting Yucatán's history. Strolling through the

Plaza Grande, visitors can enjoy the lively atmosphere, street performers, and local vendors selling traditional Yucatecan crafts and foods. Mérida is also renowned for its cultural scene. The city hosts numerous festivals, concerts, and events throughout the year, celebrating its rich heritage and vibrant arts. The Gran Museo del Mundo Maya offers an in-depth look at the Maya civilization, with extensive exhibits on their history, culture, and contributions. For a taste of local cuisine, visitors can explore the bustling markets and traditional restaurants serving dishes like cochinita pibil, panuchos, and sopa de lima.

5.3 Hidden Gems of the Yucatán

Each of these hidden gems of the Yucatán Peninsula offers a unique glimpse into the rich tapestry of the region's natural and cultural wonders. From the tranquil cenotes and ancient ruins to the charming towns and secluded beaches, these destinations promise an unforgettable journey through one of Mexico's most enchanting corners. Discovering these treasures will not only enrich your travel experience but also ignite a deep appreciation for the diverse beauty and heritage of the Yucatán Peninsula.

Xlacah: Tucked away in the heart of the Yucatán Peninsula lies the serene Cenote Xlacah, a hidden gem that promises a truly magical experience. Unlike the more frequented cenotes, Xlacah offers a tranquil escape where the crystal-clear waters create a mesmerizing dance of light and shadow. Surrounded by dense jungle, this cenote exudes an air of untouched purity, making it an ideal spot for those seeking solace and reflection. As you dip into the refreshing water, you'll feel the weight of the world lift off your shoulders, replaced by the calming embrace of nature. Swimming here feels like entering a secret sanctuary, where the ancient Maya once gathered for rituals and ceremonies.

Ek' Balam: Hidden away from the bustling crowds is Ek' Balam, a remarkable Maya archaeological site that rivals the more famous ruins but remains shrouded in mystery and allure. The name Ek' Balam, meaning "Black Jaguar," evokes the spirit of this ancient city, which is adorned with intricately carved stelae and friezes that tell tales of Maya mythology and history. Climbing to the top of the main pyramid reveals an expansive view of the surrounding jungle, a panorama that feels both exhilarating and humbling. Unlike the more tourist-heavy sites, Ek' Balam allows for a more intimate exploration of Maya culture, where you can wander through ancient plazas and temples with a sense of discovery and wonder.

Valladolid: In the heart of the Yucatán, the town of Valladolid is a hidden gem that captures the essence of colonial Mexico. Its cobblestone streets and colorful façades offer a picturesque setting that feels both nostalgic and inviting. Valladolid is not just a visual delight; it is a sensory experience, with local markets brimming with handmade crafts and vibrant textiles. The town's central plaza is a lively hub where locals and visitors alike gather to enjoy traditional music and dance. A stroll through Valladolid reveals charming cafes where you can savor delicious local cuisine, from savory cochinita pibil to sweet marquesitas.

Punta Laguna: For those who yearn for a more off-the-beaten-path beach experience, Punta Laguna offers a pristine retreat far from the crowded shores of the Yucatán. This secluded stretch of coastline is embraced by lush mangroves and fringed with powdery white sand that leads to the clear, turquoise waters of the Caribbean. Punta Laguna is a sanctuary for nature lovers, where you can spot exotic birds and playful monkeys amidst the tranquil surroundings. The area is perfect for those who seek solitude and a deeper connection with nature, offering opportunities for kayaking, snorkeling, and simply lounging by the serene waters.

5.4 Exploring the Beaches

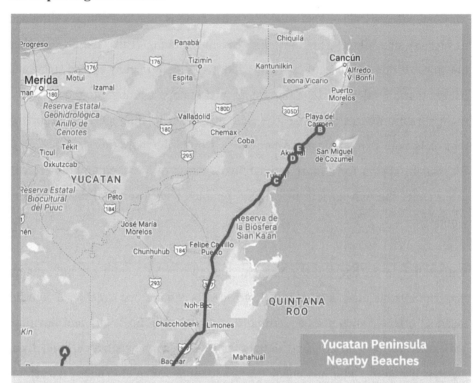

Directions from Yucatán Peninsula to Xpu Ha, Quintana Roo, Mexico

A
Yucatan Peninsula

B
Playa del Carmen, Quintana Roo, Mexico

D
Akumal, Quintana Roo, Mexico

C
Tulum, Quintana Roo, Mexico

E
Xpu Ha, Quintana Roo, Mexico

Each of these beaches on the Yucatán Peninsula offers a unique and unforgettable experience, inviting you to explore their distinct charms and discover the true essence of this captivating region. From the lively shores of Playa del Carmen to the tranquil sands of Holbox, the Yucatán's beaches are a testament to the region's unparalleled natural beauty and diverse offerings.

Playa del Carmen: Playa del Carmen is a dazzling gem on the Yucatán Peninsula's coast, where the magic of the Caribbean Sea meets the vibrant pulse of a lively town. As you step onto its soft, powdery sand, you'll immediately feel a sense of both excitement and relaxation. The beach stretches for miles, offering plenty of space to find your perfect spot. The water is a mesmerizing shade of turquoise, warm and inviting, perfect for a refreshing dip or a leisurely swim. Beyond the beach, the lively Quinta Avenida (Fifth Avenue) beckons with an array of shops, restaurants, and bars. Here, you can savor local delicacies or dance the night away. Playa del Carmen is more than a beach; it's a destination where every moment is infused with the vibrant energy of the Riviera Maya.

Tulum: Tulum offers a unique blend of natural beauty and ancient history. This beach is not just a place to relax; it's a sanctuary where you can immerse yourself in serenity while gazing at the remnants of the Maya civilization perched on the cliffs above. The beach is known for its stunning white sand and clear, azure waters that seem to stretch infinitely. The waves gently lap against the shore, creating a soothing soundtrack to your beach day. The backdrop of the Tulum ruins adds a sense of grandeur to the experience, making it feel as though you're stepping into a living postcard. Whether you're lounging in a hammock, exploring the nearby cenotes, or indulging in a beachfront massage, Tulum's charm is undeniable.

Akumal: Akumal is a picturesque bay renowned for its clear, calm waters and friendly sea turtles. Its name, which means "Place of the Turtles" in Maya, reflects the area's significance as a nesting site for these magnificent creatures. As you wade into the warm, shallow waters, you'll likely encounter sea turtles gliding gracefully beneath the surface. Snorkeling in Akumal is a magical experience, offering a chance to observe these gentle giants in their natural habitat. The beach itself is a serene haven, with soft sand and crystal-clear water. The surrounding area is tranquil and less crowded, allowing for a peaceful escape where you can connect with nature in a truly special way.

Holbox: Holbox Island, accessible only by ferry, is a slice of paradise that feels worlds away from the hustle and bustle of modern life. The beaches here are a blend of untouched beauty and tranquil solitude. The soft, white sands are bordered by warm, shallow waters that are perfect for a relaxing swim or a leisurely stroll. Holbox is known for its laid-back atmosphere, where time seems to slow down, allowing you to truly unwind. The island's beaches are often dotted with colorful beach huts and hammocks, inviting you to relax and soak in the peaceful surroundings. Holbox is also famous for its bioluminescent waters, which light up with a magical glow at night, creating a surreal and unforgettable experience.

Xpu-Ha: Xpu-Ha is a hidden treasure that offers a more secluded beach experience, away from the more tourist-heavy spots. This stretch of coastline is known for its pristine, crystal-clear waters and soft, white sand. The beach is fringed by lush palm trees, providing natural shade and adding to its tranquil ambiance. Xpu-Ha is ideal for those seeking a peaceful retreat, with ample space to find your own slice of paradise. The shallow waters make it perfect for families and snorkelers alike, offering glimpses of vibrant marine life without the crowds. The beach's unspoiled beauty and serene atmosphere make it a perfect spot to relax and rejuvenate while enjoying the natural splendor of the Yucatán Peninsula.

5.5 Dining and Nightlife in the Yucatán

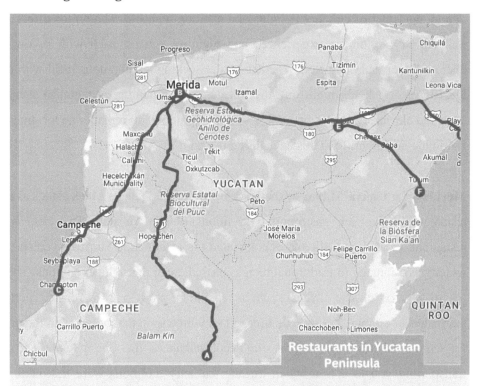

Directions from Yucatán Peninsula to Taboo | Best Beach Club Tulum, Zona Hotelera Tulum, Tulum, Quintana Roo, Mexico

A
Yucatán Peninsula

B
La Chaya Maya, Calle 57, Parque Santa Lucia, Centro, Merida, Yucatan, Mexico

C
El Cardenal, Champoton, Campeche, Mexico

D
La Vaquita, Calle 12 Norte, Centro, Playa del Carmen, Quintana Roo, Mexico

E
Cenote Zaci, Santa Ana, Valladolid, Yucatan, Mexico

F
Taboo | Best Beach Club Tulum, Zona Hotelera Tulum, Tulum, Quintana Roo, Mexico

The Yucatán Peninsula, known for its lush landscapes and ancient ruins, is also a vibrant epicenter of culinary delights and exciting nightlife. The region offers a rich tapestry of dining experiences and nightlife venues, each with its own distinct flavor and character. Whether you're seeking a sumptuous meal with a local twist or a lively night out, the Yucatán has something to tantalize every taste and elevate every evening. Here's an in-depth look at remarkable locations for dining and nightlife in this enchanting region.

Merida's La Chaya Maya: In the heart of Merida, La Chaya Maya stands as a testament to the rich gastronomic traditions of the Yucatán. This beloved restaurant, located on Calle 62, is celebrated for its authentic Yucatecan cuisine, which pays homage to traditional recipes passed down through generations. The menu features classic dishes such as cochinita pibil, a slow-roasted pork marinated in achiote, and sopa de lima, a tangy lime soup that bursts with flavor. La Chaya Maya's charming, rustic decor enhances the dining experience, transporting you to a time when Yucatán culinary traditions were first taking shape. In addition to its delectable food, La Chaya Maya offers a selection of local beverages, including refreshing agua de chaya and traditional Mexican beers. The prices are reasonably moderate, making it a great spot for both casual diners and those looking to indulge in a full Yucatán feast. The restaurant is open daily from 8:00 AM to 10:00 PM, serving breakfast, lunch, and dinner.

El Cardenal in Cancun: El Cardenal, located in the bustling Hotel Zone of Cancun, offers a sophisticated dining experience that marries traditional Mexican flavors with contemporary culinary techniques. Situated on Boulevard Kukulcán, this restaurant is renowned for its elegant setting and refined menu. The menu at El Cardenal features a blend of traditional and innovative dishes, including duck breast in a citrus sauce and seafood risotto with a hint of tequila. The restaurant's dedication to high-quality ingredients and artistic presentation ensures that each dish is a feast for both the eyes and the palate. In addition to its exquisite food, El Cardenal boasts an impressive wine list, showcasing both local Mexican wines and international selections. Prices here are on the higher end, reflecting the upscale nature of the dining experience. El Cardenal is open daily from 12:00 PM to 11:00 PM, providing a sophisticated atmosphere for both lunch and dinner.

La Vaquita in Playa del Carmen: For those seeking a lively night out, La Vaquita in Playa del Carmen offers an unforgettable blend of great food and energetic nightlife. Located on Calle 10, just a short walk from the bustling Quinta Avenida, La Vaquita is known for its fun, casual atmosphere and its impressive selection of cocktails and tacos. The menu features a variety of street food classics, including tacos al pastor, quesadillas, and nachos, all prepared with a flavorful twist. The bar at La Vaquita is a focal point of the experience, offering a wide range of cocktails, from margaritas to mojitos, as well as an extensive list of tequila and mezcal. The prices are reasonable, making it a popular spot for both locals and visitors. The venue is open from 12:00 PM to 3:00 AM, ensuring that the party continues late into the night.

Cenote Zaci in Valladolid: Cenote Zaci, located in the historic town of Valladolid, offers a dining experience that combines the natural beauty of the Yucatán with the rich flavors of local cuisine. Situated near the cenote of the same name, this restaurant offers a unique setting where diners can enjoy their meals overlooking the crystal-clear waters of the cenote. The menu features traditional Yucatecan fare, including panuchos and salbutes, as well as refreshing tropical drinks. What sets Cenote Zaci apart is its stunning location and the opportunity to dine in a truly picturesque setting. The prices are moderate, making it accessible to a wide range of visitors. The restaurant operates daily from 9:00 AM to 7:00 PM, offering breakfast, lunch, and an early dinner. Dining at Cenote Zaci provides a memorable experience, blending culinary delights with the natural splendor of one of the Yucatán's most beautiful cenotes.

Taboo in Tulum: Taboo, located on the shores of Tulum, offers a chic and sophisticated dining and nightlife experience. Situated on Carretera Tulum-Boca Paila, this stylish venue is known for its modern decor, trendy ambiance, and excellent seafood. The menu at Taboo includes a range of contemporary dishes, from sushi and ceviche to grilled seafood and gourmet pizzas. The restaurant's beachside location adds to its allure, with diners enjoying stunning views of the Caribbean Sea as they savor their meals. The bar at Taboo is equally impressive, featuring an array of craft cocktails, premium spirits, and fine wines. Prices at Taboo reflect its upscale nature, but the exceptional service and vibrant atmosphere make it worth the splurge. The venue is open daily from 12:00 PM to 2:00 AM, offering a perfect blend of fine dining and nightlife.

CHAPTER 6
EXPLORING THE PACIFIC COAST

6.1 Overview of the Pacific Coast

The Pacific Coast of Mexico is a realm where the sun kisses the ocean with golden hues and the rhythm of waves provides a soundtrack to life. From the verdant hills of Baja California to the lush jungles of Chiapas, this stretch of coastline offers an enchanting tapestry of landscapes, cultures, and adventures that beckon travelers with an irresistible allure. Imagine the Pacific Coast as a vast canvas where every sunrise paints a new masterpiece. The region begins in the north with Baja California, a peninsula that stretches like a finger into the ocean. Here, the rugged beauty of the desert meets the azure waters in a breathtaking display of contrasts. The lively city of Tijuana, just over the border from the United States, offers a vibrant mix of art, culture, and cuisine.

6.2 Must-See Attractions

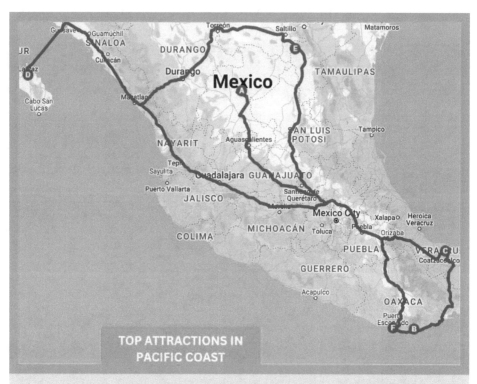

Directions from Mexico to Puerto Escondido, Oaxaca, Mexico

A Mexico	**D** La Paz, BCS, Mexico
B Santa María Huatulco, Oaxaca, Mexico	**E** Sierra Madre Oriental, Nuevo Leon, Mexico
C Los Tuxtlas, Ver., Mexico	**F** Puerto Escondido, Oaxaca, Mexico

The Pacific Coast of Mexico is a region of unparalleled beauty, rich history, and vibrant culture, offering a diverse range of attractions that cater to all types of travelers. From the modern amenities and cultural heritage of Puerto Vallarta and Acapulco to the historic charm of Mazatlán and the tranquil atmosphere of Zihuatanejo, each destination provides a unique and unforgettable experience. Exploring the Pacific Coast is a journey through stunning landscapes, vibrant cities, and authentic Mexican traditions, offering a wealth of opportunities for adventure, relaxation, and cultural immersion. Whether you are seeking a lively beach vacation, a cultural exploration, or a peaceful retreat, the Pacific Coast of Mexico has something to offer every traveler.

- 6.2.1 Puerto Vallarta

Situated between the Sierra Madre Mountains and the Pacific Ocean, Puerto Vallarta is a vibrant coastal city that offers a perfect blend of traditional Mexican charm and modern amenities. Located in the state of Jalisco, Puerto Vallarta is easily accessible by air through the Gustavo Díaz Ordaz International Airport, which serves numerous domestic and international flights. Visitors can also reach the city by bus or car, with well-maintained roads connecting it to major cities like Guadalajara and Mexico City. Puerto Vallarta is renowned for its stunning beaches, lively nightlife, and rich cultural heritage. The Malecón, a scenic boardwalk stretching along the waterfront, is a must-visit. Here, visitors can enjoy breathtaking ocean views, vibrant sculptures, street performances, and a variety of shops and restaurants. The historic Zona Romántica, with its cobblestone streets and charming colonial architecture, offers a glimpse into the city's past. The Church of Our Lady of Guadalupe, with its iconic crown-topped tower, is a prominent landmark and a testament to Puerto Vallarta's deep-rooted religious traditions.

- 6.2.2 Acapulco

Acapulco, often referred to as the "Pearl of the Pacific," is a city with a rich history and a reputation as one of Mexico's premier beach destinations. Located in the state of Guerrero, Acapulco is accessible by air through the General Juan N. Álvarez International Airport, which connects the city to major domestic and international destinations. It is also reachable by road, with a scenic highway offering stunning coastal views. Acapulco's iconic bay, with its crescent-shaped coastline, is lined with golden beaches, luxury resorts, and vibrant nightlife. One of Acapulco's most famous attractions is La Quebrada, where daring cliff divers perform breathtaking jumps from heights of up to 35 meters into the narrow ocean cove below. This thrilling spectacle is a must-see, with performances held multiple times a day. For a more relaxed experience, visitors can enjoy a sunset cruise around Acapulco Bay, offering stunning views of the coastline and the city's skyline. Acapulco also offers a variety of outdoor activities. The beaches, such as Playa Condesa and Playa Icacos, are perfect for swimming, sunbathing, and water sports.

- 6.2.3 Mazatlán

Mazatlán, known as the "Pearl of the Pacific," is a charming coastal city in the state of Sinaloa. It is renowned for its beautiful beaches, rich cultural heritage, and vibrant festivals. Mazatlán is easily accessible by air through the General Rafael Buelna International Airport, which serves numerous domestic and international flights. The city is also well-connected by bus and road to other major destinations in Mexico. Mazatlán's historic center, also known as Centro Histórico, is a delightful area with beautifully preserved 19th-century architecture. The Angela Peralta Theater, a stunning neoclassical building, hosts a variety of cultural events and performances. The Plazuela Machado, a picturesque square surrounded by cafes and restaurants, is a perfect spot to relax and soak in the city's atmosphere. The Cathedral Basilica of the Immaculate Conception, with its striking twin towers and intricate interior, is another highlight of the historic center.

- 6.2.4 Zihuatanejo

Zihuatanejo, a picturesque fishing village turned tourist destination, offers a tranquil and authentic Mexican experience. Located in the state of Guerrero, Zihuatanejo is easily accessible by air through the Ixtapa-Zihuatanejo International Airport, which serves domestic and international flights. The town is also connected by bus and road to major cities in Mexico. Zihuatanejo's charm lies in its laid-back atmosphere, stunning beaches, and friendly locals. The town's main beach, Playa La Ropa, is a beautiful stretch of white sand lined with palm trees and beachside restaurants. Visitors can relax on the beach, swim in the calm waters, or engage in water sports like kayaking and paddleboarding. The nearby Playa Las Gatas, accessible by a short boat ride, offers excellent snorkeling opportunities with its clear waters and vibrant marine life. The town's central area, with its cobblestone streets and traditional Mexican architecture, is perfect for a leisurely stroll. The fishing pier, where local fishermen bring in their daily catch, provides a glimpse into Zihuatanejo's maritime heritage.

6.3 Hidden Gems of the Pacific Coast

The Pacific Coast of Mexico is dotted with stunning locales that lie off the beaten path, each offering its own unique charm and allure. These hidden gems, often overshadowed by more famous destinations, provide a richer, more intimate experience of the coast's natural and cultural beauty. If you're looking to uncover some of Mexico's best-kept secrets, these five hidden gems will ignite your wanderlust and invite you to explore their serene wonders.

Isla de la Piedra: Just across the bay from Mazatlán, Isla de la Piedra—also known as Stone Island—is a haven of tranquility. Accessible by a short, scenic boat ride, this island feels like a step back in time, away from the hustle and bustle of the mainland. Here, palm-fringed beaches stretch out in serene splendor, offering soft sands and gentle waves that are perfect for a peaceful day of relaxation. The island's charm lies in its simplicity: small, family-run seafood shacks serve freshly caught fish and shrimp, providing an authentic taste of local cuisine. For those looking to explore, a leisurely stroll along the shoreline reveals vibrant tidal pools teeming with marine life. Isla de la Piedra is a tranquil escape where the rhythm of the ocean is the only sound you'll hear.

Yelapa: Accessible only by boat from Puerto Vallarta, Yelapa is a picturesque village hidden away in a lush tropical jungle. This secluded oasis is a paradise for nature lovers and those seeking solace from the more crowded tourist spots. Yelapa's main attraction is its stunning waterfall, which can be reached by a scenic hike through the jungle. The journey to the falls offers breathtaking views of the surrounding greenery and wildlife. Once there, the cascading waters create a natural pool perfect for a refreshing dip. Yelapa's serene beaches and charming, unspoiled environment make it a true escape into nature. The village itself, with its rustic charm and friendly locals, adds to the island's allure, creating an experience that feels both adventurous and deeply relaxing.

Costa Careyes: If you're searching for a luxurious, off-the-beaten-path destination, Costa Careyes is a hidden gem that promises exclusivity and natural beauty. Located between Puerto Vallarta and Manzanillo, Costa Careyes is renowned for its striking architecture, private villas, and pristine beaches. The area's unique blend of modern luxury and traditional Mexican design creates an atmosphere of elegance and serenity. The secluded beaches here are perfect for sunbathing, swimming, or simply enjoying the stunning ocean views. Costa Careyes also offers a range of activities, from private yacht charters to horseback riding along the beach. This destination's blend of luxury and natural beauty makes it an ideal retreat for those looking to indulge in a more exclusive experience.

San Pancho: San Pancho, officially known as San Francisco, is a small, vibrant town located a short drive north of Sayulita. Despite its modest size, San Pancho is brimming with character and charm. The town is renowned for its artistic community and vibrant cultural scene, which is reflected in its colorful murals, local art galleries, and bustling markets. The beach here, Playa San Pancho, is less crowded than its neighbors and offers a more relaxed environment for sunbathing and swimming. San Pancho is also home to a number of eco-friendly initiatives and community projects, making it a destination that feels both welcoming and meaningful. Whether you're exploring the local art scene or participating in one of the town's cultural festivals, San Pancho offers a unique and enriching experience that captures the essence of the Pacific Coast's hidden gems.

6.4 Outdoor Activities on the Pacific Coast

The Pacific Coast of Mexico is a playground for outdoor enthusiasts, offering a myriad of exhilarating activities amidst breathtaking landscapes. From surfing the world's best waves to exploring hidden waterfalls, the region invites adventurers to immerse themselves in its natural beauty and dynamic experiences. Here's a look at five thrilling outdoor activities that promise to captivate your spirit and ignite your sense of wonder.

Surfing the Epic Waves of Puerto Escondido: Known globally as the "Mexican Pipeline," Puerto Escondido's Playa Zicatela is a surfer's dream come true. Here, the Pacific Ocean's mighty swells create waves that are both formidable and mesmerizing. For experienced surfers, catching these powerful waves is a challenge that brings both thrill and satisfaction. The sight of these towering waves crashing against the shore is awe-inspiring, as is the feeling of riding them. The energy and camaraderie among the surfing community here add to the exhilarating atmosphere. Whether you're a seasoned pro or a beginner eager to learn, Puerto Escondido offers an unforgettable surfing experience, with world-class surf schools and a vibrant local scene.

Kayaking Through the Bioluminescent Waters of Huatulco: Imagine paddling through waters that sparkle with every stroke of your paddle—this magical experience awaits you in Huatulco. The bioluminescent bays here are a natural wonder, where tiny organisms light up the water in a dazzling display of blue-green glow. Kayaking through these glowing waters feels like drifting through a scene from a fantasy. The phenomenon is best experienced at night, when the contrast between the dark sky and the glowing water creates a mesmerizing effect. As you glide through this ethereal landscape, the serene and surreal experience will make you feel like you're part of something truly special. It's an otherworldly adventure that showcases the natural beauty and mystery of the Pacific Coast.

Hiking the Stunning Trails of Los Tuxtlas: For those who crave a deeper connection with nature, the Los Tuxtlas Biosphere Reserve offers some of the most spectacular hiking trails in Mexico. Located in the southern part of Veracruz, this region is a lush, tropical paradise where dense rainforests meet volcanic landscapes. The hiking trails here lead you through vibrant green canopies, past cascading waterfalls, and up to panoramic viewpoints that reveal the vast expanse of the jungle below. One of the most rewarding hikes is to the top of Volcán San Martín, where you're greeted with sweeping views of the surrounding landscape and the Pacific Ocean in the distance. The diverse flora and fauna along the trails, including exotic birds and colorful butterflies, make every step of the hike an adventure in discovery.

Snorkeling Among the Vibrant Reefs of La Paz: La Paz, nestled in Baja California Sur, is renowned for its incredible snorkeling opportunities. The azure waters of the Sea of Cortez are home to a rich underwater world, where vibrant coral reefs and marine life abound. Snorkeling in these clear waters offers a chance to swim alongside playful sea lions, encounter schools of shimmering fish, and explore the colorful coral gardens. The warm, inviting waters make it easy to spend hours underwater, marveling at the diversity and beauty of marine life. The sense of wonder as you glide through this underwater realm is unmatched, and the memories of your encounters with these oceanic wonders will stay with you long after you've left.

Zip-Lining Over the Jungle Canopy of Sierra Madre: For an adrenaline-pumping adventure, zip-lining through the jungle canopy of the Sierra Madre Mountains is a must-do. This activity provides a thrilling bird's-eye view of the lush landscape below, with cables stretched between platforms high above the forest floor. As you soar through the treetops, you'll experience the rush of the wind and the exhilarating freedom of flight. The panoramic views of the dense jungle and surrounding mountains are simply breathtaking, offering a unique perspective on the natural beauty of the region. Each zip-line segment delivers a mix of excitement and awe, making it a memorable and exhilarating way to experience the wilderness.

6.5 Dining and Nightlife on the Pacific Coast

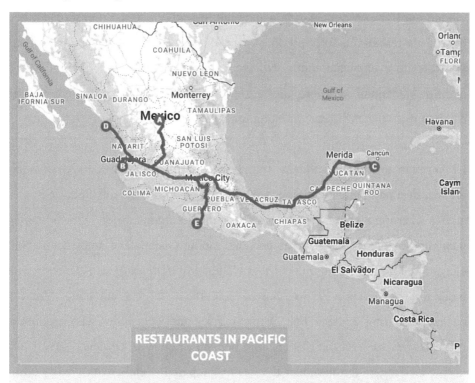

RESTAURANTS IN PACIFIC COAST

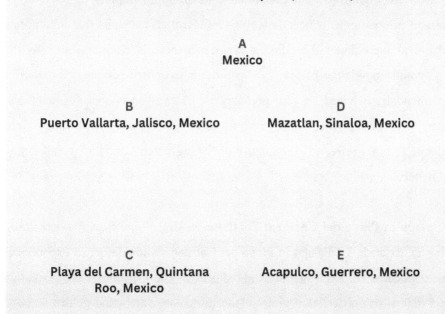

Directions from Mexico to Acapulco, Guerrero, Mexico

A
Mexico

B
Puerto Vallarta, Jalisco, Mexico

D
Mazatlan, Sinaloa, Mexico

C
Playa del Carmen, Quintana Roo, Mexico

E
Acapulco, Guerrero, Mexico

The Pacific Coast of Mexico is not only a paradise of natural beauty but also a vibrant hub for exceptional dining and nightlife experiences. From sophisticated beachfront restaurants to lively local bars, this region offers an array of options that cater to every taste and mood. Exploring these five distinctive dining and nightlife locations will provide a rich tapestry of flavors, ambiance, and entertainment that will leave a lasting impression.

El Arrayán in Puerto Vallarta: In the heart of Puerto Vallarta, El Arrayán is a premier destination that combines stunning views with exquisite dining. Situated atop a charming colonial-style building, the restaurant offers a breathtaking panorama of the city's coastline and the Pacific Ocean. The ambiance is both elegant and relaxed, with a decor that blends traditional Mexican elements with modern sophistication.El Arrayán is celebrated for its authentic Mexican cuisine, featuring a menu that showcases regional specialties with a gourmet twist. Dishes such as the tender mole poblano, rich with complex flavors and deep chocolate undertones, and the freshly prepared ceviche with a zesty citrus marinade are highlights. The restaurant also offers an impressive selection of local and international wines, as well as handcrafted cocktails that incorporate fresh, local ingredients. The dining experience here is complemented by the friendly and knowledgeable staff, who provide excellent service and can offer recommendations based on your preferences. El Arrayán is open for lunch and dinner, with hours from 12:00 PM to 11:00 PM daily. Prices range from moderate to high, reflecting the quality of the ingredients and the overall dining experience.

La Palapa in Playa del Carmen: For those seeking a quintessential beachfront dining experience, La Palapa in Playa del Carmen stands out as an exceptional choice. Located directly on the sandy shores of the Caribbean, the restaurant offers diners an unparalleled view of the turquoise waters and golden sunsets. The setting is casual yet elegant, with thatched roofs and open-air seating that creates a relaxed and inviting atmosphere. La Palapa specializes in seafood, with a menu that includes everything from freshly grilled shrimp and succulent lobster to flavorful fish tacos and refreshing ceviche. The bar serves a variety of tropical cocktails, including signature drinks like the "Palapa Margarita" and the "Mango Mojito," which perfectly complement the coastal ambiance. The restaurant's signature dish, the seafood paella, is a must-try for anyone looking to indulge in a hearty and flavorful meal. Open daily from 8:00 AM to 11:00 PM, La Palapa caters to both breakfast and dinner crowds. Prices are moderate, with most main courses ranging from $15 to $35 USD. The combination of excellent food, stunning views, and a relaxed atmosphere makes La Palapa a memorable dining destination.

Café des Artistes in Puerto Vallarta: Café des Artistes is a culinary jewel in Puerto Vallarta, renowned for its sophisticated dining experience and artistic flair. Located in a beautifully restored colonial building, the restaurant exudes an air of elegance with its intimate setting and exquisite decor. The ambiance is enhanced by soft lighting, artistic murals, and a lush garden patio that provides a serene escape from the bustling city. The menu at Café des Artistes is a fusion of international and Mexican cuisine, crafted with precision and creativity. Signature dishes include the roasted duck with a tangy tamarind glaze and the beautifully presented tuna tartare. The restaurant also boasts an extensive wine list, featuring selections from both local vineyards and renowned international producers. Cocktails are meticulously prepared, with options like the "Café Martini" and the "Mango Margarita" providing a unique twist on classic favorites. Café des Artistes is open for dinner from 6:00 PM to 11:00 PM, Monday through Saturday. Prices are on the higher side, reflecting the premium quality of the ingredients and the sophisticated dining experience. The restaurant's dedication to excellence in both food and service ensures a memorable evening out.

El Guero in Mazatlán: El Guero is a vibrant cantina in Mazatlán that embodies the lively spirit of the city's nightlife. Located in the historic center, the bar is a popular spot for both locals and visitors looking to experience authentic Mexican nightlife. The ambiance is colorful and energetic, with traditional decor, lively music, and a welcoming atmosphere that encourages socializing and enjoyment. The menu at El Guero focuses on traditional Mexican fare, including hearty dishes such as tacos al pastor, enchiladas, and quesadillas. The bar is renowned for its extensive selection of tequila and mezcal, offering patrons the chance to sample a wide range of local and artisanal spirits. Signature cocktails, such as the "Guero Margarita" and the "Mango Mezcal Mule," are crafted to complement the vibrant flavors of the cuisine. El Guero opens its doors at 4:00 PM and remains lively until late into the night, closing at 2:00 AM. Prices are very affordable, with most dishes and drinks ranging from $5 to $15 USD. The lively atmosphere, combined with the delicious food and drink options, makes El Guero a must-visit for those seeking an authentic taste of Mazatlán's nightlife.

La Bodeguita del Medio in Acapulco: La Bodeguita del Medio in Acapulco is a chic lounge that brings a touch of Havana to Mexico's Pacific Coast. Located in the heart of the city's nightlife district, the venue offers a stylish and sophisticated environment where guests can enjoy a blend of Cuban and Mexican influences. The menu at La Bodeguita del Medio offers a fusion of Cuban and Mexican dishes, with highlights including the savory ropa vieja, delicious tostones, and flavorful Mexican tacos. The bar is famous for its classic cocktails, such as the "Mojito" and the "Daiquiri," which are expertly prepared to enhance the overall dining experience. The lounge also features live music, adding to the lively and festive ambiance. Open from 6:00 PM to 1:00 AM daily, La Bodeguita del Medio provides a sophisticated yet relaxed atmosphere for evening dining and entertainment. Prices are moderate to high, with most dishes and drinks priced between $10 and $30 USD.

CHAPTER 7
DISCOVERING THE BAJA CALIFORNIA PENINSULA

7.1 Overview of Baja California

Baja California is a land where rugged landscapes meet oceanic splendor, creating an alluring destination that captures the imagination and stirs the soul. This enchanting region, stretching from the arid deserts to the azure waters of the Pacific, offers an extraordinary mix of natural beauty, vibrant culture, and unforgettable experiences. From its dramatic coastlines and picturesque towns to its rich history and outdoor adventures, Baja California is a treasure trove of exploration and wonder. The journey through Baja California begins with its captivating geography. The state is a marvel of contrasts: the Sierra de San Pedro Mártir mountain range, with its craggy peaks and panoramic vistas, stands in striking contrast to the tranquil beaches and turquoise waters of the Pacific. The stark beauty of the Baja desert, dotted with cacti and rugged terrain, meets the lush oasis of Ensenada's wine country, where rolling vineyards paint the landscape in shades of green.

7.2 Must-See Attractions

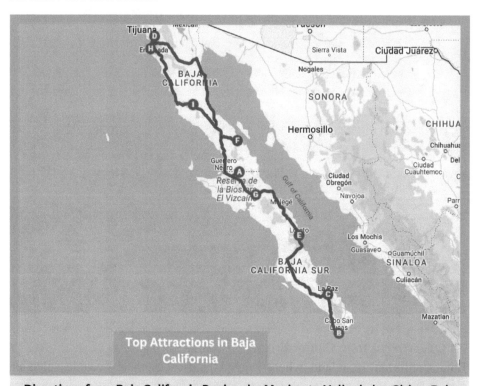

Top Attractions in Baja California

Directions from Baja California Peninsula, Mexico to Valle de los Cirios, Baja California, Mexico

A
Baja California Peninsula, Mexico

D
Valle de Guadalupe, Baja California, Mexico

G
San Ignacio, BCS, Mexico

B
Cabo San Lucas, BCS, Mexico

E
Loreto, BCS, Mexico

H
La Bufadora, Baja California, Mexico

C
La Paz, BCS, Mexico

F
Bahía de los Ángeles, Baja California, Mexico

I
Valle de los Cimos, Baja California, Mexico

Baja California is a diverse and captivating region that offers a wealth of attractions for every type of traveler. From the luxurious resorts and vibrant nightlife of Cabo San Lucas to the tranquil beaches and historic charm of Loreto, the region promises unforgettable experiences. The Valle de Guadalupe wine region invites visitors to indulge in world-class wines and gourmet cuisine, while the coastal beauty and cultural vibrancy of La Paz and Ensenada provide endless opportunities for adventure and relaxation. Whether seeking outdoor thrills, cultural enrichment, or simply a serene escape, Baja California's must-see attractions ensure a memorable journey through one of Mexico's most enchanting destinations. One of the most compelling features of Baja California is its coastline, which is nothing short of breathtaking. The area around La Paz, the state capital, showcases some of the most pristine and stunning beaches in Mexico. The gentle waves of Balandra Beach, with its clear, shallow waters and dramatic rock formations, create an almost surreal paradise that invites relaxation and reflection. Nearby, the stunning waters of the Sea of Cortez teem with marine life, making it a haven for snorkeling and diving enthusiasts. The sight of playful sea lions and colorful fish swimming in the crystalline depths is an experience that will leave you in awe of nature's wonders.

- 7.2.1 Cabo San Lucas

Cabo San Lucas, at the southern tip of the Baja California Peninsula, is a vibrant destination known for its stunning beaches, luxury resorts, and thrilling nightlife. Easily accessible by air through the Los Cabos International Airport, it is well connected to major cities in the United States, Canada, and other parts of Mexico. Visitors can also reach Cabo San Lucas by car via the Transpeninsular Highway or by sea on various cruise lines.

The iconic Arch of Cabo San Lucas, also known as El Arco, is a natural rock formation that marks the meeting point of the Pacific Ocean and the Sea of Cortez. Boat tours provide a close-up view of this breathtaking landmark, along with opportunities for snorkeling and spotting marine life such as sea lions and whales. The lively Marina district is a hub of activity, offering a variety of shops, restaurants, and bars, making it perfect for both daytime exploration and nighttime entertainment. Cabo San Lucas is a paradise for outdoor enthusiasts. Its beaches, such as Medano Beach, are perfect for swimming, sunbathing, and water sports like jet skiing and parasailing. For a more secluded experience, Chileno Beach offers excellent snorkeling with its clear waters and abundant marine life. Adventure seekers can embark on deep-sea fishing excursions, ATV tours, or zip-lining through the desert landscapes. Golfers will find world-class courses designed by renowned architects, set against stunning ocean and desert backdrops.

- 7.2.2 La Paz

La Paz, the capital of Baja California Sur, offers a more laid-back and authentic Mexican experience compared to the bustling resort towns. Located along the Sea of Cortez, La Paz can be reached by air through the Manuel Márquez de León International Airport or by ferry from Mazatlán and Topolobampo. The city is also accessible by car via the Transpeninsular Highway.La Paz is known for its serene beaches, crystal-clear waters, and abundant marine life. Playa Balandra, with its shallow turquoise waters and stunning rock formations, is often considered one of the most beautiful beaches in Mexico. Visitors can enjoy swimming, kayaking, and paddleboarding in this tranquil bay. Another popular spot is Playa Tecolote, offering a more active beach experience with water sports, beachfront restaurants, and stunning views of Espiritu Santo Island. Espiritu Santo Island, a UNESCO World Heritage Site, is a must-visit for nature lovers. Accessible by boat tours from La Paz, the island offers opportunities for snorkeling, diving, and wildlife watching. Visitors can swim with sea lions, observe colorful fish and coral reefs, and spot various bird species. The island's pristine beaches and rugged landscapes make it a perfect destination for eco-tourism and outdoor adventures.

- 7.2.3 Valle de Guadalupe Wine Region

The Valle de Guadalupe Wine Region, located in the northern part of Baja California, is Mexico's premier wine-producing area. Easily accessible by car from Tijuana, Ensenada, and other nearby cities, the region is renowned for its picturesque vineyards, award-winning wines, and gourmet cuisine. Valle de Guadalupe's Mediterranean-like climate, with warm days and cool nights, creates ideal conditions for growing a variety of grapes. The region is home to numerous wineries, ranging from small family-owned vineyards to large, internationally recognized estates. Visitors can enjoy wine tastings, vineyard tours, and learn about the winemaking process from knowledgeable vintners. The region's signature wines include robust reds, crisp whites, and innovative blends that reflect the unique terroir.

- 7.2.4 Loreto

Loreto, one of the oldest towns in Baja California Sur, is a charming destination with a rich history, stunning natural beauty, and a relaxed coastal vibe. Located on the eastern coast of the Baja Peninsula along the Sea of Cortez, Loreto can be reached by air through the Loreto International Airport, which has connections to major Mexican cities and select U.S. destinations. The town is also accessible by car via the Transpeninsular Highway. Loreto's historic significance dates back to its founding in 1697 as the first Spanish settlement on the Baja Peninsula. The town's historic center features well-preserved colonial architecture, including the Mission of Our Lady of Loreto, the oldest mission in Baja California. The mission, with its beautiful baroque facade and peaceful courtyard, offers a glimpse into the region's colonial past and religious heritage. The adjacent Museo de las Misiones showcases artifacts and exhibits related to the Jesuit missions and indigenous cultures.

7.3 Hidden Gems of Baja California

Baja California, with its rugged landscapes and dramatic coastlines, is a land of hidden treasures waiting to be discovered. While many are drawn to its well-known destinations, the real magic often lies in its lesser-known corners. These hidden gems, tucked away from the usual tourist routes, offer an authentic and captivating glimpse into the region's true essence. Each location presents a unique blend of natural beauty, cultural richness, and serene solitude, promising experiences that will enchant and inspire.

Bahía de los Ángeles: On the eastern shore of the Baja California Peninsula, Bahía de los Ángeles is a tranquil oasis that captures the heart of anyone who ventures there. This remote bay, sheltered by the rugged mountains and arid landscapes, is a haven for those seeking peace away from the bustling crowds. The pristine waters of the bay, with their shimmering turquoise hues, invite you to dive into a world of marine wonder. Snorkeling here reveals a vibrant underwater world teeming with colorful fish, sea turtles, and graceful rays. What makes Bahía de los Ángeles truly special is its isolation and the warmth of its small, welcoming community. The local fishing village exudes a rustic charm, with its simple wooden structures and traditional lifestyle. Here, you can savor freshly caught seafood, enjoy breathtaking sunsets over the bay, and embrace the slow-paced rhythm of life. The serene beauty of this hidden gem provides a perfect retreat for those looking to reconnect with nature and escape the everyday hustle.

San Ignacio: Deep in the heart of Baja California's desert landscape lies the enchanting San Ignacio Lagoon, a place where time seems to stand still. This hidden gem is renowned for its unparalleled whale watching opportunities. Every winter, gray whales migrate to the warm, sheltered waters of the lagoon to give birth and nurture their young. Witnessing these majestic creatures up close, as they breach and play in the crystal-clear waters, is a profoundly moving experience. San Ignacio Lagoon is surrounded by a picturesque desert landscape, where ancient palms and serene waters create a striking contrast. The area is also home to a wealth of birdlife, making it a paradise for birdwatchers and nature enthusiasts.

La Bufadora: Just south of Ensenada, La Bufadora is a spectacular natural phenomenon that often flies under the radar of many visitors. This blowhole, located on the rugged coastline, is one of the largest of its kind in the world. When the ocean waves crash into the narrow opening, they create a powerful jet of water that shoots high into the air, creating a dramatic and thunderous display. The sheer force and spectacle of La Bufadora are awe-inspiring, and the surrounding cliffs provide stunning views of the Pacific Ocean. The area around La Bufadora is dotted with quaint shops and local eateries where you can sample Baja's culinary delights. The charm of the location, combined with the thrilling natural spectacle, makes La Bufadora a must-visit for those seeking a unique and exhilarating experience on the Pacific Coast.

Valle de los Cirios: Venturing inland from the coast, the Valle de los Cirios presents a surreal and otherworldly landscape that feels like stepping onto another planet. This remote valley, located in the heart of Baja California's desert, is known for its bizarre and fascinating flora, including the towering cirio cacti that give the valley its name. These colossal cacti, with their otherworldly shapes and sizes, create a landscape that is both mesmerizing and mysterious. The vast, barren expanse of Valle de los Cirios is perfect for those who appreciate solitude and the stark beauty of desert landscapes. The area offers opportunities for hiking, photography, and exploration, with the chance to witness stunning sunsets and star-filled skies. The enigmatic allure of Valle de los Cirios makes it a hidden gem that invites you to explore its otherworldly terrain and experience the raw beauty of Baja California's desert wilderness.

Loreto's Hidden Beaches: While Loreto is known for its charming colonial architecture and historical significance, it also boasts a series of hidden beaches that are well worth discovering. These secluded spots, accessible only by boat or rugged trails, offer serene escapes from the more frequented areas. Beaches like Playa Ensenada Blanca and Playa Ligüí are known for their soft, golden sands and crystal-clear waters, perfect for swimming, snorkeling, and relaxing in complete tranquility. The calm, turquoise waters of these hidden beaches are ideal for kayaking and paddleboarding, providing a peaceful way to explore the coastal beauty of the region. The absence of crowds and the pristine natural setting make these beaches a perfect retreat for those seeking solitude and an intimate connection with Baja California's coastal charm.

7.4 Outdoor Adventures in Baja California

Baja California's Pacific Coast is a realm where nature's grandeur and the spirit of adventure intertwine, offering experiences that transcend the ordinary. From the rugged beauty of desert landscapes to the shimmering allure of the Pacific Ocean, this region is a playground for outdoor enthusiasts. Each adventure promises a unique blend of excitement and natural splendor, inviting travelers to explore some of the most breathtaking and exhilarating spots on the Pacific Coast.

Whale Watching in the Laguna San Ignacio: In the heart of Baja California's desert, the Laguna San Ignacio is a sanctuary where the majestic gray whales come to give birth and nurture their young. The experience of whale watching here is nothing short of magical. From December to April, these magnificent creatures migrate from the Arctic to the warm, sheltered waters of the lagoon. Boarding a boat and venturing into the lagoon, you'll witness the awe-inspiring sight of these gentle giants breaching and playing in their natural habitat. The tranquility of the lagoon, with its mirror-like waters reflecting the surrounding desert landscape, creates a surreal backdrop for this extraordinary encounter. As you watch the whales' playful displays, their immense size and grace become even more awe-inspiring. The intimacy of the experience, combined with the stunning scenery, makes whale watching in Laguna San Ignacio an unforgettable adventure that connects you with one of nature's most incredible phenomena.

Snorkeling in the Sea of Cortez: Known as the "Aquarium of the World," the Sea of Cortez is a haven for underwater adventures. The crystal-clear waters teem with marine life, from vibrant coral reefs to playful sea lions and an array of colorful fish. Snorkeling in this pristine environment offers a chance to immerse yourself in a world of vibrant colors and dynamic marine ecosystems. The area around La Paz and Cabo Pulmo National Park is particularly renowned for its excellent snorkeling opportunities.

Kayaking in Bahía de los Ángeles: Bahía de los Ángeles, with its tranquil bay and stunning coastal scenery, is an ideal location for kayaking. Paddling through the serene waters allows you to explore hidden coves, rocky outcrops, and secluded beaches that are otherwise inaccessible. The calm, shallow waters of the bay are perfect for a leisurely kayaking experience, offering an intimate connection with the landscape. As you glide across the surface, you might spot dolphins darting through the water, or glimpse the colorful marine life below.

Hiking the Sierra de San Pedro Mártir: For those seeking a high-altitude adventure, the Sierra de San Pedro Mártir offers dramatic landscapes and invigorating hikes. This mountain range, which rises up from the desert floor, provides a stark contrast to Baja California's coastal areas. The hiking trails here traverse a variety of terrains, from lush pine forests to rugged rocky outcrops, each offering panoramic views of the surrounding landscapes.

7.5 Dining and Nightlife in Baja California

Restaurants in Baja Calirfornia

Directions from Baja California Peninsula, Mexico to El patio, Cuauhtémoc, San Miguel neighborhood, Mexico City, CDMX, Mexico

A
Baja California Peninsula, Mexico

C
Pier 7 Restaurant Bar, Mulegé Mission, River Zone, Tijuana, Baja California, Mexico

B
Natal Coffee, Natal, Lindavista, Mexico City, CDMX, Mexico

D
The patio, Cuauhtémoc, San Miguel neighborhood, Mexico City, CDMX, Mexico

Baja California, a region known for its striking landscapes and vibrant culture, also boasts a rich tapestry of dining and nightlife experiences that captivate both locals and visitors alike. From upscale seafood restaurants to lively bars, each location offers a unique glimpse into the culinary and social life of this fascinating region. Here, we delve into five standout spots that exemplify Baja California's diverse and exciting dining and nightlife scene, providing a taste of the local flavor and a glimpse into the region's vibrant atmosphere.

Café de Ciudad: In the heart of Ensenada, Café de Ciudad is a charming eatery that captures the essence of Baja California's culinary innovation. This café, renowned for its fusion of traditional Mexican flavors with contemporary twists, offers a delightful menu that ranges from fresh seafood dishes to inventive vegetarian options. The highlight of the menu includes their signature Baja fish tacos, which are a local favorite, featuring perfectly crisped fish paired with a zesty cabbage slaw and homemade salsa. For those seeking something more substantial, the grilled octopus with garlic and chili offers a taste of Baja's coastal bounty. The drink menu at Café de Ciudad is equally impressive, featuring a selection of artisanal cocktails and local craft beers. The café's margaritas, made with freshly squeezed lime juice and a variety of flavored infusions, are particularly popular. The ambiance of Café de Ciudad is both relaxed and sophisticated, with an inviting decor that combines rustic charm with modern elegance. The café opens for lunch at 11 AM and serves dinner until 10 PM, making it an ideal spot for a leisurely meal or a night out with friends. The combination of exceptional food, creative drinks, and a welcoming atmosphere ensures that Café de Ciudad is a must-visit for anyone exploring Ensenada.

La Fonda de Rigo: In the bustling city of Tijuana, La Fonda de Rigo stands as a beacon of traditional Mexican cuisine. Located in a vibrant neighborhood known for its eclectic food scene, this restaurant offers a menu steeped in regional flavors and time-honored recipes. The standout dishes at La Fonda de Rigo include their succulent carne asada, which is marinated to perfection and grilled over an open flame, and the rich, flavorful pozole, a traditional Mexican stew that captures the essence of comfort food. The restaurant's bar serves a range of classic Mexican cocktails, including refreshing micheladas and robust tequila-based drinks. La Fonda de Rigo's interior is a celebration of Mexican culture, adorned with colorful murals and traditional decor that create a lively and festive atmosphere. The restaurant opens its doors for lunch at 12 PM and continues serving dinner until midnight, making it a great spot for both a casual lunch and a late-night feast. The combination of authentic flavors and a vibrant setting makes La Fonda de Rigo a true gem in Tijuana's culinary landscape.

Baleen: For those seeking a more upscale dining experience, Baleen in La Paz offers an exquisite blend of fine dining and breathtaking ocean views. Situated along the waterfront, Baleen specializes in gourmet seafood, with a menu that highlights the freshest catches from the Sea of Cortez. The restaurant's signature dishes include the seared scallops with saffron risotto and the lobster tail grilled to perfection, each showcasing the rich flavors of the region's seafood. The drink menu at Baleen features an impressive selection of fine wines and expertly crafted cocktails, with a focus on local and international options that complement the sophisticated menu. The ambiance of Baleen is elegant and refined, with floor-to-ceiling windows that provide stunning views of the harbor and the surrounding sea. The restaurant opens for dinner at 6 PM and closes at 11 PM, making it an ideal choice for a romantic evening or a special celebration. The combination of exquisite cuisine, top-notch service, and panoramic views ensures that Baleen offers a dining experience that is both memorable and luxurious.

Muelle 7: In the coastal town of Rosarito, Muelle 7 offers a vibrant nightlife experience with its lively atmosphere and dynamic entertainment. Located right on the beach, this popular bar and restaurant provides a casual and fun environment where guests can enjoy a range of delectable dishes and refreshing drinks. The menu features a variety of seafood options, including ceviche and shrimp tacos, as well as hearty favorites like burgers and nachos. Muelle 7's bar is known for its creative cocktails and extensive selection of local and international beers. The venue also hosts live music and DJ sets, creating an energetic and festive ambiance that makes it a favorite spot for locals and tourists alike. The beachside location allows for stunning sunset views, adding to the overall experience. Muelle 7 opens in the afternoon and stays open until late into the night, ensuring that it is a prime destination for those looking to enjoy a lively evening by the ocean.

El Patio: For a more laid-back and cozy dining experience, El Patio in San Quintín provides a charming and intimate setting that highlights Baja California's culinary heritage. Located in a quaint neighborhood, this restaurant offers a menu filled with traditional Mexican dishes, including hearty mole enchiladas and tender carnitas. The emphasis on homemade, flavorful dishes creates a warm and inviting atmosphere that feels like a home away from home. The bar at El Patio serves a range of classic Mexican beverages, from frosty cervezas to expertly crafted margaritas. The restaurant's decor is a blend of rustic and contemporary elements, creating a cozy and relaxed environment that is perfect for enjoying a leisurely meal. El Patio opens for lunch at 1 PM and serves dinner until 9 PM, making it an ideal spot for a relaxed afternoon or early evening dining experience. The combination of delicious food, friendly service, and a cozy atmosphere makes El Patio a cherished spot for anyone visiting San Quintín.

CHAPTER 8
EXPLORING THE COLONIAL HEARTLAND

8.1 Overview of the Colonial Heartland

The Colonial Heartland of Mexico is a region where history and tradition intertwine, offering a rich tapestry of experiences that transport visitors to a bygone era of opulence and cultural flourish. Situated in the heart of the country, this area is a testament to Mexico's colonial past, where each cobblestone street, grand plaza, and baroque façade tells a story of a time when Spanish influence sculpted the landscape and left an indelible mark on its identity. As you step into the Colonial Heartland, the ambiance is immediately palpable. The air seems to hum with a blend of history and romance, as if each corner holds a secret waiting to be discovered. Cities like Guanajuato, San Miguel de Allende, and Querétaro emerge as shimmering jewels in this historical crown, each offering its unique charm and allure. These cities are renowned for their well-preserved colonial architecture, vibrant arts scenes, and the warm, welcoming spirit of their residents.

8.2 Must-See Attractions

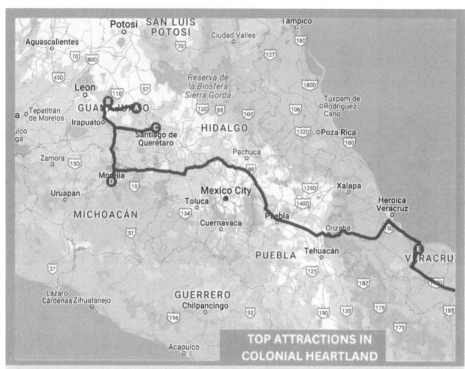

Directions from San Miguel de Allende, Guanajuato, Mexico to Yucatan Peninsula

A
San Miguel de Allende,
Guanajuato, Mexico

D
Morelia, Michoacan, Mexico

B
Guanajuato, Mexico

E
Tlacotalpan, Veracruz, Mexico

C
Querétaro, Qro., Mexico

F
Yucatan Peninsula

The Colonial Heartland of Mexico is a region rich in history, culture, and natural beauty. From the artistic charm of San Miguel de Allende to the vibrant history of Guanajuato, the blend of modernity and tradition in Querétaro, and the colonial grandeur of Morelia, each destination offers unique experiences and unforgettable memories. Exploring these must-see attractions in the Colonial Heartland provides a deeper understanding of the region's rich cultural heritage and ensures a truly enriching travel experience. Guanajuato, with its labyrinthine alleys and colorful facades, feels almost like a living museum. The city's dramatic landscape, carved into the hillsides, gives it an almost otherworldly quality. Here, the maze of streets leads to hidden plazas, each one a delightful surprise. The city's festivals, such as the San Miguel de Allende Music Festival, offer a vibrant celebration of art and culture against a backdrop of historical splendor.

- 8.2.1 San Miguel de Allende

San Miguel de Allende, often hailed as one of the most enchanting towns in Mexico, is a gem nestled in the heart of the Colonial Heartland. Located in the central state of Guanajuato, it is about a three-hour drive from Mexico City, making it an accessible destination for both international and domestic travelers. This UNESCO World Heritage site is renowned for its well-preserved colonial architecture, vibrant arts scene, and captivating cultural heritage. The town's focal point is the Parroquia de San Miguel Arcángel, a neo-Gothic church whose pink limestone towers dominate the skyline. The church's intricate facade and towering spires make it a popular subject for photographers and a must-see for visitors. Surrounding the church is the Jardín Principal, a lively square where locals and tourists alike gather to enjoy live music, street performances, and the town's vibrant atmosphere. A visit to the Mercado de Artesanías provides an opportunity to explore stalls filled with handcrafted jewelry, textiles, and other artisanal goods. For a deeper understanding of the local culture, the Casa de Cultura Banamex hosts exhibitions, workshops, and performances that celebrate the region's artistic and cultural heritage.

- 8.2.2 Guanajuato

Guanajuato, the capital city of the state bearing the same name, is a vibrant and historic destination that captivates visitors with its colorful buildings, winding alleyways, and rich cultural heritage. Situated in a picturesque valley, Guanajuato is about an hour and a half drive from San Miguel de Allende and is easily accessible by bus or car. One of the city's most iconic landmarks is the

Teatro Juárez, a stunning 19th-century theater that hosts a variety of cultural events, including music concerts, theatrical performances, and film screenings. The theater's grand facade, with its Doric columns and statues of Greek muses, is a testament to the city's cultural sophistication.

The city's historic center is a labyrinth of narrow streets and underground tunnels, making it a delight to explore on foot. The Basilica of Our Lady of Guanajuato, with its striking yellow facade and baroque interior, is a must-visit, as is the Alhóndiga de Granaditas, a historic granary that played a crucial role in Mexico's fight for independence. Guanajuato is also home to the famous Callejón del Beso, or Alley of the Kiss, a narrow alleyway where legend has it that lovers who kiss on the third step will be blessed with seven years of happiness.

- 8.2.3 Querétaro

Querétaro, a city that beautifully marries its colonial heritage with contemporary charm, is a vibrant destination in central Mexico. Located about three hours northwest of Mexico City, Querétaro is easily reachable by bus, car, or a short flight. Its historic center, a UNESCO World Heritage site, is a treasure trove of colonial architecture, bustling plazas, and cultural landmarks. The Aqueduct of Querétaro, an impressive 18th-century structure with 74 arches, is one of the city's most iconic landmarks. This engineering marvel provided the city with water and stands as a testament to the architectural prowess of the colonial era.

Visitors can enjoy a scenic walk along the aqueduct or take in the views from one of the nearby parks.

The Plaza de Armas, the city's main square, is surrounded by beautiful colonial mansions, bustling cafés, and important historical sites. The Casa de la Corregidora, now the state government palace, played a crucial role in the Mexican War of Independence. Visitors can explore the building and learn about its historical significance through exhibits and guided tours. Querétaro is also known for its vibrant arts and culture scene. The Museo de Arte de Querétaro, housed in a stunning former convent, features an impressive collection of colonial and contemporary art. The city hosts numerous festivals throughout the year, including the Querétaro International Film Festival and the Santiago de Querétaro Fair, which celebrate local and international arts, crafts, and cuisine.

- 8.2.4 Morelia

Morelia, the capital of the state of Michoacán, is a city that transports visitors back in time with its well-preserved colonial architecture and rich historical legacy. Located about four hours west of Mexico City, Morelia is accessible by bus, car, or a short flight. The city's historic center, a UNESCO World Heritage site, is a stunning showcase of pink stone buildings, grand cathedrals, and charming plazas. The Morelia Cathedral, with its imposing twin towers and intricate Baroque facade, is the city's most iconic landmark. The cathedral's interior is equally impressive, featuring stunning altars, beautiful frescoes, and a magnificent organ. The Plaza de Armas, located in front of the cathedral, is a lively square where visitors can enjoy local food, street performances, and the vibrant atmosphere of the city. The Aqueduct of Morelia, an impressive 18th-century structure with 253 arches, is another must-see landmark. The aqueduct provided the city with water and stands as a testament to the architectural ingenuity of the colonial era. Visitors can enjoy a scenic walk along the aqueduct or take in the views from one of the nearby parks.

8.3 Hidden Gems of the Colonial Heartland

Beneath the well-trodden paths of Mexico's Gulf Coast lies a treasure trove of hidden gems that captivate the imagination and beckon the adventurous traveler. These secluded spots, often overshadowed by their more famous counterparts, offer a glimpse into the untouched beauty and authentic culture of this vibrant region. From serene natural wonders to charming historical enclaves, the Gulf Coast's hidden gems promise to enrich your journey with unique experiences and unforgettable memories.

Tuxpan Mangroves: In the coastal town of Tuxpan, Veracruz, the mangroves present a world of tranquil wonder that remains largely undiscovered by the masses. This lush, green labyrinth of waterways and dense foliage is a sanctuary for countless bird species and offers a serene escape from the bustling tourist spots. As you glide through the winding channels by boat, the rhythmic sound of your oar slicing through the water is the only interruption to the natural symphony of chirping birds and rustling leaves. The mangroves are a haven for wildlife enthusiasts and nature lovers, offering a rare opportunity to witness the delicate ecosystem in action. The best time to explore this hidden paradise is during the early morning or late afternoon when the light casts a magical glow over the water and the wildlife is most active.

Isle of Sacrificio: A short boat ride from the bustling port city of Veracruz leads you to the tranquil Isle of Sacrificio, an island steeped in both historical significance and natural beauty. Once a site of ancient rituals and sacrifices, this small island now serves as a serene retreat with pristine beaches and crystal-clear waters. The island's name, which translates to "Sacrifice," hints at its rich cultural past, but today, it offers a peaceful escape for those seeking solitude and natural beauty.

Tlacotalpan: Tlacotalpan, a UNESCO World Heritage site located just inland from the Gulf Coast, is a charming town that exudes a timeless quality. Known for its vibrant, pastel-colored buildings and cobblestone streets, Tlacotalpan offers a glimpse into a bygone era. The town's historic center is adorned with colonial architecture, and its lively market is a feast for the senses with stalls selling fresh produce, local crafts, and traditional foods. Tlacotalpan's annual Candelaria Festival is a highlight, where the streets come alive with music, dance, and colorful parades. Visiting Tlacotalpan feels like stepping into a living history book, where the past and present blend seamlessly in a celebration of Mexican culture.

Yucatán Peninsula: The Yucatán Peninsula is renowned for its cenotes—natural sinkholes filled with clear, turquoise water. While many cenotes are well-known tourist spots, there are lesser-known, hidden cenotes that offer a more intimate and secluded experience. One such hidden gem is the Cenote Xcanche, located near the small town of the same name. This cenote is surrounded by lush jungle and offers a serene setting for swimming, snorkeling, or simply relaxing on the water's edge. The cenote's crystal-clear waters and dramatic underwater rock formations make it a hidden paradise for those seeking adventure away from the crowds. Exploring these hidden cenotes allows you to connect with the natural beauty of the Yucatán and experience its refreshing and mysterious allure.

Celestún: Celestún, a small fishing village located on the western edge of the Yucatán Peninsula, is home to one of Mexico's most enchanting natural reserves—the Celestún Biosphere Reserve. This expansive wetland is renowned for its mangroves, salt flats, and rich birdlife, including the iconic flamingos that flock to the area during the winter months. While many visitors head to the reserve's main viewing spots, the tranquil shores of Celestún offer a more peaceful and intimate experience.

8.4 Historical and Cultural Tours

The Colonial Heartland of Mexico is a realm where history and culture intertwine seamlessly, offering travelers a chance to delve deeply into the past while embracing the vibrant present. This region, characterized by its stunning colonial architecture and rich traditions, is a treasure trove of historical and cultural experiences that promise to enchant and educate. Embarking on a journey through these meticulously crafted tours provides an unparalleled opportunity to explore the heart of Mexico's colonial legacy and immerse oneself in its enduring charm.

San Miguel de Allende: San Miguel de Allende, with its enchanting streets and artistic spirit, offers a historical and cultural tour that transports visitors to a bygone era. Begin at the Parroquia de San Miguel Arcángel, the town's iconic neo-Gothic church that dominates the skyline with its striking pink spires. The church's intricate facade and its role in the town's history provide a captivating introduction to San Miguel's rich heritage. From the Parroquia, meander through the narrow, cobblestone streets of the historic center, where each turn reveals a new chapter in the town's story. The Casa de Allende, the former home of Ignacio Allende, a key figure in Mexico's War of Independence, is a must-visit. This well-preserved colonial residence has been converted into a museum, offering a profound glimpse into the life and times of this revolutionary hero.

Querétaro's Historical Chronicles: Querétaro, a city steeped in historical significance, offers a tour that delves into its role in Mexico's journey to independence. Start at the Convent of San Francisco, a serene and beautifully restored building that reflects the architectural elegance of the colonial period. The convent's cloisters and chapels provide a quiet, reflective space where visitors can appreciate the craftsmanship and devotion of the era. The tour continues to the Teatro de la República, a grand theater where the Treaty of Guadalupe Hidalgo was signed, ending the Mexican-American War.

Dolores Hidalgo: Dolores Hidalgo, a town of immense historical significance, invites visitors to explore its role as the cradle of Mexican independence. Begin with a visit to the Museo de la Independencia, located in the former residence of Miguel Hidalgo. The museum's exhibits and artifacts provide a detailed account of the events leading up to Mexico's fight for independence and the key figures involved. Wander through the town's central plaza, where you can admire the historic architecture and enjoy the lively atmosphere of local markets.

San Luis Potosí and the Huasteca Potosina: San Luis Potosí, a city with a rich colonial past, offers a tour that combines historical exploration with natural beauty. Begin in the city's historic center, where the Teatro de la Paz stands as a testament to the region's cultural heritage. The theater's elegant architecture and vibrant cultural scene provide a window into San Luis Potosí's artistic legacy.

8.5 Dining and Nightlife in the Colonial Heartland

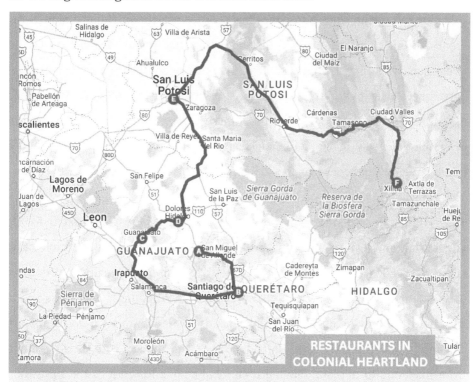

Directions from San Miguel de Allende, Guanajuato, Mexico to Huasteca Potosina, Xilitla, Cd Valles, San Luis Potosi, Mexico

A
San Miguel de Allende, Guanajuato, Mexico

D
Dolores Hidalgo, Guanajuato, Mexico

B
Queretaro's Municipal Pantheon, Cimatario, Santiago de Querétaro, Qro., Mexico

E
San Luis Potosí, San Luis Potosí, Mexico

C
Guanajuato, Mexico

F
Huasteca Potosina, Xilitla, Cd Valles, San Luis Potosi, Mexico

The Colonial Heartland of Mexico is not only renowned for its historical splendor and picturesque landscapes but also for its vibrant dining and nightlife scenes. From charming eateries that showcase traditional Mexican cuisine to lively bars where local culture comes alive, this region offers a rich tapestry of experiences that invite visitors to indulge in both culinary delights and spirited nightlife. Embark on a journey through these captivating locations that promise to enrich your stay in the Colonial Heartland, each offering a unique glimpse into the region's gastronomic and social life.

San Miguel de Allende: San Miguel de Allende, a town celebrated for its artistic flair and historical charm, presents Café Rama as a prime example of its culinary excellence. Each dish is crafted with precision and creativity, reflecting the restaurant's dedication to both innovation and tradition. The ambiance is warm and inviting, with a decor that blends rustic charm with contemporary elegance. Café Rama is open daily for lunch and dinner, with prices ranging from moderate to upscale, making it an ideal choice for both casual meals and special occasions. For an evening of vibrant socializing and stunning views, The Rooftop Bar offers an unparalleled experience. Perched atop one of San Miguel's historic buildings, this bar provides panoramic views of the town's skyline and the surrounding countryside.

Querétaro: In Querétaro, the dining scene combines rich tradition with innovative flair, exemplified by La Mariposa. This restaurant, renowned for its elegant ambiance and exquisite cuisine, offers a menu that celebrates both Mexican and international influences. Guests can savor dishes like the tender pork belly with citrus glaze or the rich chocolate tamal, each crafted with meticulous attention to detail. The restaurant's refined decor and attentive service create an atmosphere that is both sophisticated and welcoming. La Mariposa is a favorite for special occasions and romantic dinners, with prices reflecting its upscale offerings. The restaurant is open for lunch and dinner, making it a versatile choice for any dining experience. For those seeking a lively and authentic taste of Querétaro's nightlife, El Mesón de Chucho stands out as a quintessential destination. This traditional cantina embodies the spirit of Mexican social life with its vibrant music, colorful decor, and extensive selection of local spirits. Patrons can enjoy classic Mexican dishes such as chiles en nogada and barbacoa, paired with refreshing cocktails and local beers. The lively atmosphere is enhanced by live mariachi performances, creating an immersive experience that captures the essence of Mexican celebration. El Mesón de Chucho is open daily from 3 PM to 1 AM, offering a lively and festive setting for a night out on the town.

Dolores Hidalgo: In Dolores Hidalgo, a town steeped in historical significance, La Casa de Doña Emma offers a dining experience that reflects the region's rich cultural heritage. This restaurant, housed in a beautifully restored colonial building, serves traditional Mexican fare with a focus on local ingredients. Dishes such as the slow-cooked carnitas and the hand-made corn tortillas highlight the restaurant's commitment to authentic and flavorful cuisine. The charming decor, featuring traditional Mexican motifs and handcrafted furnishings, enhances the dining experience, creating a warm and inviting atmosphere. La Casa de Doña Emma is open daily for lunch and dinner, with prices that are both reasonable and reflective of the high-quality ingredients used in their dishes. For a taste of Dolores Hidalgo's vibrant nightlife, El Reloj provides a lively setting where locals and visitors can enjoy traditional music, delicious food, and refreshing drinks.

CHAPTER 9
DISCOVERING THE GULF COAST

9.1 Overview of the Gulf Coast

The Gulf Coast of Mexico unfurls as a captivating mosaic of natural beauty, cultural richness, and endless adventure, offering an enchanting escape for those seeking to immerse themselves in a region where every sunrise paints a new chapter of discovery. Stretching from the verdant landscapes of Veracruz to the sun-kissed shores of Tabasco, the Gulf Coast is a treasure trove of experiences waiting to be unearthed. At its heart, the Gulf Coast is a realm where lush tropical rainforests meet azure waters, creating a stunning contrast that is as visually arresting as it is serene. The coastlines, lined with pristine beaches, invite travelers to bask in the sun's warm embrace, while the gentle lapping of waves against the shore provides a rhythmic soundtrack to lazy afternoons.

9.2 Must-See Attractions

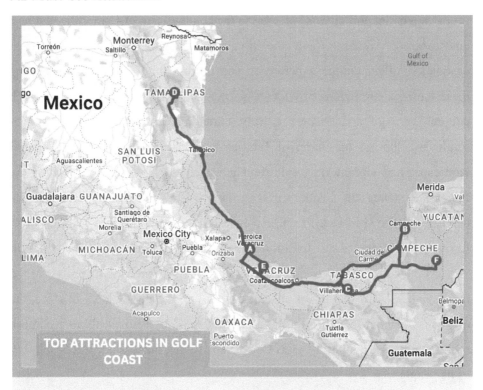

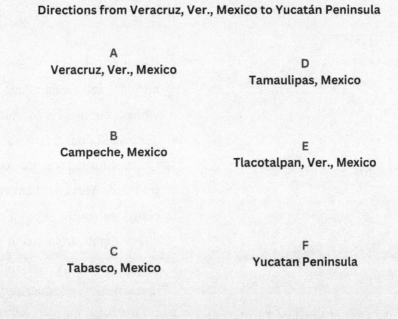

Directions from Veracruz, Ver., Mexico to Yucatán Peninsula

A
Veracruz, Ver., Mexico

D
Tamaulipas, Mexico

B
Campeche, Mexico

E
Tlacotalpan, Ver., Mexico

C
Tabasco, Mexico

F
Yucatan Peninsula

The Gulf Coast of Mexico is a region rich in history, culture, and natural beauty. From the vibrant port city of Veracruz to the colonial gem of Campeche, the lush landscapes of Tabasco, and the diverse attractions of Tamaulipas, each destination offers unique experiences and unforgettable memories. Exploring these must-see attractions provides a deeper understanding of the region's rich cultural heritage and ensures a truly enriching travel experience. Moving southward, the coastal charm of Tabasco beckons with its enchanting natural landscapes and vibrant local culture. The region's lush wetlands, including the famous Pantanos de Centla, offer a haven for birdwatchers and wildlife enthusiasts. The Gulf Coast's cultural tapestry is further enriched by its colorful festivals and vibrant local traditions. From the lively Carnival celebrations in Veracruz, where the streets come alive with music, dance, and parades, to the traditional festivals that honor ancient customs and celebrate local folklore, the region is a vibrant stage for cultural expression. Each festival offers a glimpse into the heart and soul of the Gulf Coast, showcasing the warmth and hospitality of its people.

- 9.2.1 Veracruz

Veracruz, a city steeped in history and brimming with vibrant culture, is a must-see destination on Mexico's Gulf Coast. Situated on the eastern coast of Mexico, Veracruz is easily accessible by air, with direct flights from major cities like Mexico City and Houston, or by road via a scenic drive along the Gulf of Mexico. This bustling port city is known for its rich colonial heritage, lively festivals, and stunning coastal scenery. One of the city's most iconic landmarks is the Malecón, a scenic waterfront promenade that stretches along the Gulf coast. Visitors can stroll along the Malecón, taking in views of the sparkling waters and watching the bustling activity of the port. The promenade is lined with restaurants, cafes, and shops, offering a perfect spot to enjoy local seafood dishes, such as the famous "Huachinango a la Veracruzana" (Veracruz-style red snapper), while soaking up the lively atmosphere.

- 9.2.2 Campeche

Campeche, the capital of the state of the same name, is a beautifully preserved colonial city that transports visitors back in time. Located on the western shore of the Yucatán Peninsula, Campeche is easily accessible by air, with flights from major cities like Mexico City and Cancún, or by road via a scenic drive through the Yucatán Peninsula. The city's historic center, a UNESCO World Heritage site, is a stunning showcase of colonial architecture and colorful facades. Visitors can explore the narrow, cobblestone streets lined with brightly painted buildings, many of which house charming cafes, boutique hotels, and artisan shops. The city walls, originally built to protect against pirate attacks, still stand today, offering a glimpse into Campeche's rich history. One of the city's most iconic landmarks is the Cathedral of Our Lady of the Immaculate Conception, a magnificent Baroque-style cathedral that dominates the main square, Plaza de la Independencia.

- 9.2.3 Tabasco

Tabasco, a state known for its lush landscapes and rich cultural heritage, offers visitors a unique blend of natural beauty and historical significance. Located in southeastern Mexico, Tabasco is easily accessible by air, with flights from major cities like Mexico City and Cancún, or by road via a scenic drive through the Gulf Coast region. The state capital, Villahermosa, is a vibrant city that serves as a gateway to the region's many attractions. One of the city's most popular landmarks is the Parque Museo La Venta, an open-air museum that showcases the ancient Olmec civilization. The museum's collection includes colossal stone heads, intricate sculptures, and other artifacts that provide fascinating insights into this ancient culture. For nature enthusiasts, the Pantanos de Centla Biosphere Reserve is a must-visit. This vast wetland area is home to a diverse array of wildlife, including crocodiles, manatees, and hundreds of species of birds. Visitors can explore the reserve on guided boat tours, which offer opportunities to spot wildlife and learn about the region's unique ecosystems.

- 9.2.4 Tamaulipas

Tamaulipas, a state located on the northeastern coast of Mexico, offers visitors a blend of rich history, vibrant culture, and stunning natural beauty. The state is easily accessible by air, with flights from major cities like Mexico City and Monterrey, or by road via a scenic drive along the Gulf Coast. The state capital, Ciudad Victoria, is a charming city that serves as a gateway to the region's many attractions. One of the city's most popular landmarks is the Tamaulipas Cultural

Center, which houses a museum, theater, and art gallery. The center's exhibits provide fascinating insights into the region's history and cultural heritage, while the theater hosts performances of music, dance, and theater throughout the year. For a taste of Tamaulipas' natural beauty, a visit to the El Cielo Biosphere Reserve is a must. This UNESCO-designated reserve is home to a diverse array of wildlife, including jaguars, pumas, and hundreds of species of birds. Visitors can explore the reserve on guided tours, which offer opportunities to hike through lush forests, spot wildlife, and enjoy stunning views of the surrounding mountains. Tamaulipas is also known for its rich culinary traditions, with dishes such as "cabrito" (roast goat) and "tacos de camarón" (shrimp tacos) offering a taste of the region's unique flavors. The state's bustling markets, such as the Mercado de Ciudad Victoria, provide an opportunity to sample local delicacies and purchase handmade crafts.

9.3 Hidden Gems of the Gulf Coast

Beneath the well-trodden paths of Mexico's Gulf Coast lies a treasure trove of hidden gems that captivate the imagination and beckon the adventurous traveler. These secluded spots, often overshadowed by their more famous counterparts, offer a glimpse into the untouched beauty and authentic culture of this vibrant region. From serene natural wonders to charming historical enclaves, the Gulf Coast's hidden gems promise to enrich your journey with unique experiences and unforgettable memories.

Tuxpan Mangroves: In the coastal town of Tuxpan, Veracruz, the mangroves present a world of tranquil wonder that remains largely undiscovered by the masses. This lush, green labyrinth of waterways and dense foliage is a sanctuary for countless bird species and offers a serene escape from the bustling tourist spots. As you glide through the winding channels by boat, the rhythmic sound of your oar slicing through the water is the only interruption to the natural symphony of chirping birds and rustling leaves. The mangroves are a haven for wildlife enthusiasts and nature lovers, offering a rare opportunity to witness the delicate ecosystem in action. The best time to explore this hidden paradise is during the early morning or late afternoon when the light casts a magical glow over the water and the wildlife is most active.

Isle of Sacrificio: A short boat ride from the bustling port city of Veracruz leads you to the tranquil Isle of Sacrificio, an island steeped in both historical significance and natural beauty. Once a site of ancient rituals and sacrifices, this small island now serves as a serene retreat with pristine beaches and crystal-clear waters. The island's name, which translates to "Sacrifice," hints at its rich cultural past, but today, it offers a peaceful escape for those seeking solitude and natural beauty. The island's beaches are perfect for a quiet day of sunbathing or snorkeling among the vibrant marine life. The gentle lapping of the waves against the shore and the panoramic views of the Gulf make it a hidden gem for relaxation and reflection.

Tlacotalpan: Tlacotalpan, a UNESCO World Heritage site located just inland from the Gulf Coast, is a charming town that exudes a timeless quality. Known for its vibrant, pastel-colored buildings and cobblestone streets, Tlacotalpan offers a glimpse into a bygone era. The town's historic center is adorned with colonial architecture, and its lively market is a feast for the senses with stalls selling fresh produce, local crafts, and traditional foods. Tlacotalpan's annual Candelaria Festival is a highlight, where the streets come alive with music, dance, and colorful parades. Visiting Tlacotalpan feels like stepping into a living history book, where the past and present blend seamlessly in a celebration of Mexican culture.

Celestún: Celestún, a small fishing village located on the western edge of the Yucatán Peninsula, is home to one of Mexico's most enchanting natural reserves—the Celestún Biosphere Reserve. This expansive wetland is renowned for its mangroves, salt flats, and rich birdlife, including the iconic flamingos that flock to the area during the winter months. While many visitors head to the reserve's main viewing spots, the tranquil shores of Celestún offer a more peaceful and intimate experience. Here, you can explore the picturesque beaches, take a boat tour through the mangroves, and enjoy the serene beauty of this protected area. The village itself is a charming place to sample fresh seafood and experience the laid-back lifestyle of the Gulf Coast's coastal communities.

9.4 Outdoor Activities on the Gulf Coast

The Gulf Coast of Mexico, with its blend of serene beaches, lush mangroves, and vibrant ecosystems, is an outdoor enthusiast's paradise. This stretch of coastline offers a myriad of activities that allow visitors to immerse themselves in nature, discover hidden gems, and experience the region's rich biodiversity. Whether you're seeking tranquil escapes or thrilling adventures, the Gulf Coast has something to captivate every outdoor lover's imagination.

Sailing Through the Mangroves of Tuxpan: In Tuxpan, Veracruz, the mangroves create a labyrinth of green wonder that beckons explorers to navigate its serene waterways. A sailing tour through these mangrove forests is akin to stepping into a living, breathing postcard. As you drift quietly through the winding channels, the dense foliage and the reflections dancing on the water create a mesmerizing experience. The mangroves are alive with the sounds of chirping birds and the occasional splash of wildlife, making each turn an opportunity for discovery. Guided tours often include a stop at small, hidden islands where you can take in the view and soak up the peaceful ambiance. The gentle sway of the boat, coupled with the verdant surroundings, makes this a unique and calming adventure for those seeking a connection with nature.

Snorkeling in the Crystal-Clear Waters of Isla de Sacrificio: A short boat ride from Veracruz brings you to Isla de Sacrificio, a tranquil island renowned for its crystal-clear waters and vibrant marine life. Here, snorkeling reveals an underwater world teeming with colorful fish and intriguing coral formations. The island's clear waters offer excellent visibility, allowing snorkelers to fully appreciate the diverse marine ecosystem. As you glide through the water, you'll be greeted by schools of tropical fish darting among the corals, creating a vivid tapestry of colors. The experience of snorkeling in such pristine conditions is both exhilarating and serene, offering a rare chance to explore a largely untouched marine environment.

Kayaking Through the Celestún Biosphere Reserve: Celestún, located on the western edge of the Yucatán Peninsula, is home to the Celestún Biosphere Reserve, a sanctuary of mangroves, salt flats, and diverse birdlife. Kayaking through this reserve offers a unique perspective on its ecological wonders. As you paddle through the tranquil waters, you'll encounter a variety of bird species, including the iconic flamingos that flock to the reserve during the winter months. The mangrove channels are peaceful and offer a serene backdrop for observing the natural beauty of the reserve. The gentle rhythm of paddling, combined with the sounds of nature, creates a deeply immersive experience that highlights the reserve's ecological significance.

Beachcombing and Relaxation on the Shores of Veracruz: While the Gulf Coast is known for its natural wonders and outdoor adventures, sometimes the simplest pleasures are the most rewarding. The beaches of Veracruz offer expansive stretches of golden sand where visitors can unwind and reconnect with nature. Beachcombing along these shores is a delightful way to discover seashells, driftwood, and other treasures washed ashore. The rhythmic sound of the waves and the gentle sea breeze provide a calming ambiance, making it the perfect setting for relaxation. Whether you're lounging in the sun, taking a leisurely stroll, or simply enjoying the view, the beaches of Veracruz offer a quintessential beach experience that celebrates the natural beauty of the Gulf Coast.

9.5 Dining and Nightlife on the Gulf Coast

The Gulf Coast of Mexico is not just a haven of natural beauty but also a vibrant culinary and nightlife landscape that offers a rich tapestry of flavors, experiences, and unforgettable moments. From tantalizing seafood feasts to lively night spots, the region's dining and nightlife scenes are as diverse and captivating as its landscapes. Exploring these local treasures will introduce you to the heart and soul of Gulf Coast culture, leaving you with memories that linger long after the last bite and sip.

La Parroquia in Veracruz: La Parroquia, an iconic establishment in Veracruz, is more than just a restaurant—it's a culinary institution. This historic venue, celebrated for its signature coffee and delectable pastries, offers a taste of Veracruz's rich heritage. The café's ambiance, marked by its classic decor and charming courtyard, provides a warm and inviting setting for enjoying breakfast or a leisurely afternoon coffee. The "Café Lechero," a local specialty featuring coffee with steamed milk, is a must-try, paired perfectly with fresh pan dulce. La Parroquia is not only a place to enjoy delicious food and beverages but also a cultural landmark where locals and visitors alike come together to savor the essence of Veracruz's culinary traditions.

Club Social de la Habana: For those looking to immerse themselves in the lively nightlife of the Gulf Coast, Club Social de la Habana in Coatzacoalcos is the place to be. This energetic nightclub is renowned for its pulsating music, vibrant atmosphere, and dynamic dance floor. With its Latin rhythms and an eclectic mix of genres, the club offers an exhilarating experience for both locals and visitors. The venue features live bands and DJs who keep the energy high into the early hours, while the well-crafted cocktails and expertly prepared tapas provide the perfect accompaniment to a night of dancing and socializing. Whether you're a seasoned dancer or just looking to soak up the lively ambiance, Club Social de la Habana promises an unforgettable night out.

Restaurante Villa Rica in Tampico: In the coastal city of Tampico, Restaurante Villa Rica stands out as a premier destination for seafood lovers. With its elegant setting and refined menu, this restaurant offers a sophisticated dining experience that showcases the best of Gulf Coast cuisine. The menu features a range of exquisitely prepared dishes, including the renowned "Ceviche de Campechana," a flavorful seafood cocktail bursting with fresh ingredients and tangy citrus. The restaurant's stylish decor and impeccable service create a welcoming atmosphere where guests can enjoy a leisurely meal while savoring the rich flavors of the region. Whether you're celebrating a special occasion or simply indulging in a sumptuous meal, Restaurante Villa Rica provides an exceptional dining experience that highlights the culinary excellence of Tampico.

La Bamba in Ciudad del Carmen: For a more relaxed yet equally delightful dining and nightlife experience, La Bamba in Ciudad del Carmen offers a charming blend of comfort and conviviality. This casual eatery and bar is a favorite among locals for its laid-back atmosphere and hearty, flavorful dishes. The menu features a variety of options, from savory grilled meats and seafood to delicious Mexican street food. The relaxed, open-air setting and friendly service make La Bamba an ideal spot for unwinding after a day of exploration. As the sun sets, the restaurant transforms into a lively gathering place where patrons can enjoy live music, cocktails, and the warm ambiance of the Gulf Coast.

CHAPTER 10
THE HIGHLANDS AND CENTRAL MEXICO

10.1 Overview of Central Mexico

Central Mexico, with its vibrant blend of historical richness and cultural vibrancy, offers an alluring tapestry of experiences that beckon travelers to delve deeper into the essence of this fascinating region. Spanning from the ancient ruins of indigenous civilizations to the bustling, modern cities, Central Mexico is a place where the past and present dance in a seamless harmony, creating a landscape that is both captivating and invigorating. At the heart of Central Mexico lies the state of Guanajuato, renowned for its picturesque colonial cities and rich mining history. The city of Guanajuato, a UNESCO World Heritage site, is a maze of narrow streets, colorful buildings, and hidden alleys that invite exploration. This city, with its storied past of silver mining and revolutionary significance, offers a unique charm that can be felt in its lively festivals, like the Festival Cervantino, and its atmospheric underground tunnels.

10.2 Must-See Attractions

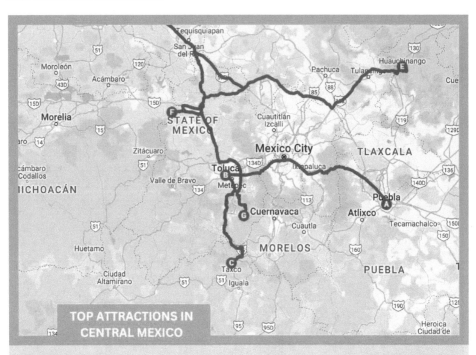

Directions from Puebla, Mexico to Valle de Bravo, State of Mexico, Mexico

A Puebla, Mexico	**E** Huauchinango, Puebla, Mexico
B Toluca, State of Mexico, Mexico	**F** El Oro, State of Mexico, Mexico
C Taxco, Guerrero, Mexico	**G** Malinalco, State of Mexico, Mexico
D Mineral de Pozos, Guanajuato, Mexico	**H** Valle de Bravo, State of Mexico, Mexico

Central Mexico is a region of remarkable diversity and rich cultural heritage, offering visitors an array of experiences that cater to every interest. From the colonial charm and culinary delights of Puebla to the eternal spring and historic allure of Cuernavaca, the natural beauty and cultural riches of Toluca, the silver legacy and picturesque streets of Taxco, and the historic heart and modern pulse of Querétaro, each destination promises unique and unforgettable memories. Exploring these must-see attractions in Central Mexico provides a deeper understanding of the region's history, culture, and natural beauty, ensuring a truly enriching travel experience. The city's cuisine, particularly its famous mole poblano, offers a culinary journey that reflects its diverse cultural influences. Puebla's streets are filled with vibrant markets and historic buildings, each telling a story of the city's evolution over centuries.

- 10.2.1 Puebla

Puebla, in the central highlands of Mexico, is a city that seamlessly blends its rich colonial heritage with modern vibrancy. Located just two hours southeast of Mexico City, Puebla is easily accessible by bus, car, or a short domestic flight. Its historic center, a UNESCO World Heritage site, boasts more than 2,600 colonial-era buildings, offering a visual feast for architecture enthusiasts. One of Puebla's most iconic landmarks is the Puebla Cathedral, an architectural marvel with its towering twin bell towers and elaborate interior. Nearby, the Rosary

Chapel in the Church of Santo Domingo is a stunning example of Baroque artistry, with its intricate gold leaf decorations and detailed frescoes. The city's Zócalo, or main square, is a lively hub where visitors can enjoy street performances, local cuisine, and the vibrant atmosphere of daily life.

- 10.2.2 Cuernavaca

Cuernavaca, known as the "City of Eternal Spring" due to its pleasant year-round climate, is a charming destination located just an hour and a half south of Mexico City. This easy accessibility makes it a popular getaway for both locals and tourists seeking a tranquil retreat from the bustling capital. Cuernavaca's most famous landmark is the Palace of Cortés, a fortress built by the Spanish conquistador Hernán Cortés in the 16th century. Today, it houses the Cuauhnáhuac Regional Museum, which features exhibits on the region's history, from pre-Hispanic times through the Mexican Revolution.

- 10.2.3 Toluca

Toluca, the capital of the State of Mexico, is a city that combines natural beauty with rich cultural offerings. Located about an hour and a half west of Mexico City, Toluca is accessible by bus, car, or a short domestic flight. Its high-altitude setting provides a cool climate and stunning mountain scenery, making it an ideal destination for nature lovers and cultural explorers alike. One of Toluca's most striking landmarks is the Cosmovitral Botanical Garden, housed in a former market building adorned with stunning stained-glass windows. These vibrant windows, designed by artist Leopoldo Flores, depict the cosmic struggle between good and evil, creating a mesmerizing backdrop for the lush botanical displays within. The garden features a wide variety of plant species from around the world, arranged in beautifully landscaped sections.

- 10.2.4 Taxco

Taxco, a picturesque town located about two and a half hours southwest of Mexico City, is renowned for its colonial architecture and rich silver mining heritage. Perched on a hillside, Taxco's narrow cobblestone streets, whitewashed houses with red-tiled roofs, and charming plazas create a timeless, romantic atmosphere. The Santa Prisca Church, an exquisite example of Baroque architecture, dominates the town's skyline. Built in the 18th century by silver magnate José de la Borda, the church's intricate facade and lavish interior are a testament to the wealth generated by Taxco's silver mines. Inside, visitors can admire the ornate altars, stunning frescoes, and detailed woodwork that make this church a true architectural gem. Taxco's reputation as a silver town is well-earned, with numerous workshops and stores offering a wide variety of handcrafted silver jewelry and decorative items. The town hosts the annual National Silver Fair, attracting artisans and buyers from across Mexico and beyond. Visitors can learn about the silver-making process, from mining to finished product, and even try their hand at crafting their own pieces in workshops offered by local artisans.

10.3 Hidden Gems of Central Mexico

Central Mexico is a region rich with well-trodden paths and celebrated destinations, yet it also holds a treasure trove of hidden gems that offer unique and deeply personal experiences. These lesser-known locales provide a chance to delve into the heart of Mexican culture and history, far from the usual tourist trails. Exploring these hidden treasures reveals the region's true essence, offering moments of discovery that resonate long after your journey has ended.

Mineral de Pozos: Tucked away in the state of Guanajuato, Mineral de Pozos is a captivating ghost town that embodies the enigmatic charm of Central Mexico's mining past. Once a bustling center of silver extraction in the 16th century, this now-abandoned town is a fascinating canvas of crumbling buildings and ancient mines. Walking through the deserted streets of Mineral de Pozos feels like stepping back in time, where the echoes of its prosperous days still whisper through the ruins.

Huauchinango: In the lush highlands of Puebla, the charming town of Huauchinango remains a hidden gem, enveloped in verdant landscapes and steeped in local traditions. Known for its stunning natural beauty and vibrant floral displays, Huauchinango is a haven for nature lovers and those seeking tranquility. The town's annual flower festival, held in November, transforms Huauchinango into a kaleidoscope of colors and scents, celebrating the region's rich horticultural heritage. Visitors can explore the nearby waterfalls, such as Cascada de las Brisas, which offer breathtaking views and refreshing escapes. The warm hospitality of Huauchinango's residents and its picturesque scenery make it a perfect retreat for those seeking an authentic and peaceful Mexican experience.

Malinalco: Perched in the lush mountains of the state of Mexico, the ancient ruins of Malinalco offer a captivating glimpse into the region's pre-Hispanic past. This archaeological site, once a ceremonial center of the Aztec empire, is renowned for its impressive rock-carved temple and stunning views of the surrounding valley. The Temple of the Jaguars, with its intricate carvings and commanding presence, stands as a testament to the spiritual and artistic achievements of the Aztec civilization. The site's serene setting and historical significance provide a profound connection to Mexico's ancient cultures. Exploring Malinalco is a journey through time, offering insights into the spiritual and artistic expressions of the Aztecs amidst breathtaking natural beauty.

Valle de Bravo: Valle de Bravo, often overshadowed by its more famous neighbors, is a picturesque village nestled around a stunning lake in the state of Mexico. This charming destination combines natural beauty with a vibrant local culture, offering a serene escape from the hustle and bustle of city life. The lake, with its tranquil waters and surrounding forests, provides ample opportunities for outdoor activities such as sailing, kayaking, and hiking. The village itself is characterized by its colonial architecture, colorful markets, and cozy restaurants that serve up delicious local cuisine. Valle de Bravo's relaxed ambiance and scenic surroundings make it an ideal spot for unwinding and experiencing the quintessential charm of Central Mexico.

10.4 Outdoor Adventures in Central Mexico

Central Mexico, a region brimming with diverse landscapes and rich cultural heritage, offers a tapestry of outdoor adventures that promise to ignite the spirit of exploration in any traveler. From the rugged mountains to serene lakes and verdant forests, the outdoor experiences in this region are as varied as they are exhilarating. These adventures invite you to engage with Central Mexico's natural beauty and embrace the thrill of discovery in some of the most captivating settings the country has to offer.

Hiking the Sierra Gorda Biosphere Reserve: In the heart of Querétaro, the Sierra Gorda Biosphere Reserve stands as a testament to Mexico's rich biodiversity and breathtaking landscapes. This vast natural haven is a paradise for hikers and nature enthusiasts, offering a network of trails that weave through diverse ecosystems, from lush rainforests to arid deserts. The reserve's rugged terrain, dramatic canyons, and cascading waterfalls create a dynamic backdrop for outdoor adventures. One of the most enchanting hikes leads to the stunning Puente de Dios (God's Bridge), a natural rock arch carved by centuries of water flow. The journey to this majestic formation, with its turquoise pools and serene environment, is an experience that captures the essence of the Sierra Gorda's untouched beauty. Hiking here is not just an adventure but a chance to connect with the profound tranquility and splendor of Mexico's wilderness.

Exploring the Lakes of Valle de Bravo: Valle de Bravo, a picturesque town encircling a stunning lake, offers a serene escape into nature's embrace. The lake itself is a playground for a myriad of water-based activities. Kayaking on the calm waters of the lake allows for a tranquil exploration of the surrounding landscapes, while sailing offers a more exhilarating experience as you glide across the reflective surface. For those who prefer to stay on land, the nearby trails offer excellent opportunities for hiking and mountain biking. The scenic vistas from these trails provide panoramic views of the lake and the encircling forests, creating a perfect backdrop for outdoor adventures. Valle de Bravo's combination of water sports and hiking makes it an ideal destination for those seeking both relaxation and adventure amidst nature's beauty.

Caving in the Grutas de Cacahuamilpa: The Grutas de Cacahuamilpa, located in Guerrero, present a subterranean adventure that is as awe-inspiring as it is exhilarating. These vast caves, formed over millennia, boast a labyrinth of chambers adorned with stunning stalactites and stalagmites. A guided tour through the caves reveals the intricate formations and geological wonders hidden within. The play of light and shadow, coupled with the ethereal beauty of the underground formations, creates a sense of wonder and exploration. For those seeking an adventurous experience that goes beyond the surface, the Grutas de Cacahuamilpa offer a unique opportunity to delve into the depths of Mexico's natural wonders, discovering a world that is both mysterious and mesmerizing.

Mountain Biking in the Sierra Madre Oriental: The Sierra Madre Oriental, a majestic mountain range that stretches through several states in Central Mexico, is a haven for mountain biking enthusiasts. The range's diverse terrain, which includes steep ascents, rugged trails, and breathtaking descents, provides a thrilling challenge for riders of all levels. Trails such as those around the town of Huauchinango offer a mix of technical obstacles and scenic beauty, allowing bikers to navigate through dense forests, cross rivers, and enjoy panoramic views of the surrounding valleys.

10.5 Dining and Nightlife in Central Mexico

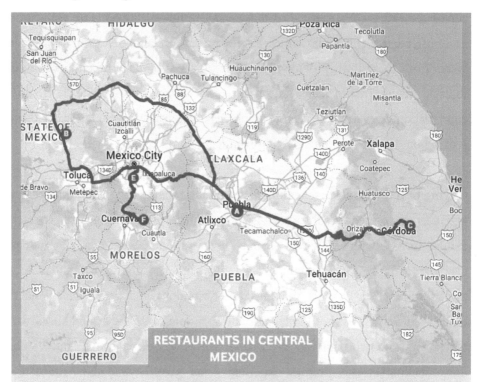

Directions from Puebla, Mexico to La Palapa, Morelos, Mexico

A
Puebla, Mexico

D
La Casa del Mendrugo, Calle 4
Sur, Centro, Puebla, Mexico

B
Lavanda Café & Brunch, México,
State of Mexico, Mexico

E
El Reloj, Mexico City, CDMX,
Mexico

C
La Mariposa, Ver., Mexico

F
La Palapa, Morelos, Mexico

Central Mexico, with its vibrant cities and charming towns, offers a rich tapestry of dining and nightlife experiences that are as diverse as the region itself. From lively markets to sophisticated eateries and spirited bars, each location presents a unique glimpse into the local culture, culinary traditions, and vibrant nightlife.

San Miguel de Allende's "Lavanda Cafe": In the heart of San Miguel de Allende, Lavanda Cafe is more than just a dining spot; it's a celebration of local ingredients and culinary artistry. This charming cafe, set in a quaint colonial building adorned with vibrant murals and lush plants, offers a menu that harmoniously blends traditional Mexican flavors with contemporary twists. Each dish is a work of art, from the tantalizing mole poblano, rich with deep, complex flavors, to the refreshing ceviche, brimming with the zest of freshly squeezed lime and vibrant herbs.

Querétaro's "La Mariposa": In the heart of Querétaro, La Mariposa stands as a beacon of traditional Mexican cuisine with a modern flair. This restaurant, renowned for its dedication to preserving authentic recipes while embracing contemporary presentation, offers a dining experience that is both nostalgic and innovative. The menu features an array of dishes that celebrate regional ingredients, such as the tender barbacoa, slow-cooked to perfection, and the delectable enchiladas queretanas, enveloped in a rich, savory sauce.

Puebla's "La Casa del Mendrugo": For those seeking a blend of history, culture, and vibrant nightlife, La Casa del Mendrugo in Puebla offers an unforgettable experience. This historic bar, set in a beautifully restored colonial mansion, combines traditional Mexican charm with a lively, modern twist. The menu features an array of tapas and small plates, perfect for sharing over cocktails and conversation.

CHAPTER 11
IMMERSING IN MEXICAN CULTURE

11.1 Festivals and Events

Mexico, a country renowned for its rich cultural tapestry and spirited traditions, comes alive with festivals and events that captivate the senses and stir the soul. Each celebration is a reflection of the country's diverse heritage and offers an unparalleled glimpse into its vibrant soul. From ancient rituals to modern festivities, Mexico's calendar is brimming with experiences that promise to enchant and inspire. Here are some of the most compelling festivals and events that showcase the nation's cultural brilliance.

Day of the Dead: In early November, Mexico transforms into a vibrant canvas of color and light during the Day of the Dead (Día de los Muertos). This UNESCO-recognized tradition, celebrated on November 1st and 2nd, is not merely a day of remembrance but a profound celebration of life. Cities like Oaxaca, Mexico City, and Patzcuaro become focal points for this magnificent festival. Families create elaborate altars adorned with marigolds, sugar skulls, and candles to honor their deceased loved ones. The streets come alive with parades featuring elaborately decorated floats and participants dressed as skeletons, embodying a joyous spirit rather than mourning.

Cancun International Music Festival: Every March, the pristine beaches of Cancun set the stage for the Cancun International Music Festival. This event is a paradise for music lovers, offering a diverse lineup of genres ranging from electronic dance to Latin rhythms. Held over a weekend, the festival attracts both international and local artists, creating an electrifying atmosphere that resonates with the sound of waves and music. The festival's location, with its stunning beachfront backdrop, provides a unique experience where attendees can dance under the stars with the Caribbean Sea as their companion. Ticket prices vary depending on the lineup and accommodations, but they generally range from $100 to $300 for a full weekend pass.

Fiestas de la Candelaria: In early February, Mexico City comes alive with the Fiestas de la Candelaria, a celebration that blends religious devotion with vibrant festivities. Held on February 2nd, the festival centers around the Candlemas Day, honoring the presentation of Jesus at the temple. The streets are adorned with colorful decorations, and there are lively parades featuring traditional dances and music. One of the festival's most cherished traditions is the sharing of tamales and atole, a warm corn-based drink, which symbolizes community and hospitality.

Festival Internacional Cervantino: Every October, the city of Guanajuato hosts the Festival Internacional Cervantino, a cultural extravaganza named in honor of the famed Spanish writer Miguel de Cervantes. This month-long festival, held throughout October, features a remarkable array of performances, including theater, dance, music, and visual arts. Artists from around the globe gather to showcase their talents, making it one of Latin America's most prestigious cultural events. The festival transforms Guanajuato into a vibrant stage, with performances taking place in various venues, from historic theaters to outdoor plazas. Entry to many events is free, though some performances or workshops may require purchasing tickets, which typically range from $10 to $50.

11.2 Mexican Folk Traditions

Traveling through Mexico is like stepping into a living, breathing museum where every corner holds a rich story of tradition and heritage. From the vibrant festivals to the deeply rooted customs, the Mexican folk traditions offer an immersive experience that resonates with authenticity and emotion. Here's a glimpse into captivating folk traditions that promise to enchant and inspire visitors.

The Charro Days Fiesta: The Charro Days Fiesta, celebrated in Matamoros, Tamaulipas, in late February, brings the essence of Mexican cowboy culture to life. This vibrant festival features charro competitions, parades, and traditional music that highlight the skills and traditions of Mexico's cowboys, or charros. The event is characterized by its colorful costumes, horseback riding exhibitions, and folkloric dances. The festival's open-air nature means that many events are free, though some ticketed activities or special seating options may be priced between $15 and $50, providing a taste of the festive atmosphere.

Guelaguetza: Held annually in Oaxaca during the last two weeks of July, the Guelaguetza festival is a vibrant celebration of Oaxacan culture. This festival, which dates back to pre-Hispanic times, is a tribute to community sharing and unity. During the event, the city is abuzz with traditional dances, music, and a dazzling display of indigenous costumes. The festival's highlight is the Guelaguetza, a series of performances featuring dances from the eight regions of Oaxaca, each with its unique rhythm and style. Visitors can also indulge in the region's culinary delights, including tlayudas and mezcal. While the main festivities are free, access to certain performances or reserved seating may require purchasing tickets, which typically range from $20 to $50.

The Tlahualilo Horse Parade: In the small town of Tlahualilo, Durango, a unique tradition unfolds in early December—the Tlahualilo Horse Parade. This local celebration is a testament to rural Mexican life, where horse enthusiasts and local families come together for a grand parade featuring elaborately decorated horses, traditional music, and lively festivities. The event is a visual feast, with each horse decked out in vibrant, hand-crafted decorations. Attending the parade is typically free, but visitors may find opportunities to support local artisans and vendors, making this tradition a heartfelt experience rooted in community spirit.

11.3 Arts and Music Scene

Mexico's arts and music scene is a mesmerizing tapestry woven with threads of tradition, innovation, and vibrant cultural expression. Each corner of this rich and diverse country offers a unique experience that promises to captivate and inspire. Whether you're strolling through the bustling streets of Mexico City or exploring the coastal charm of Cancún, the cultural heartbeat of Mexico is alive and pulsating with creativity and passion.

The Enchanting Palaces of Mexico City: In the heart of Mexico City, the Palacio de Bellas Artes stands as a beacon of artistic splendor. This opulent building, adorned with a blend of Art Nouveau and Art Deco styles, is not just a visual masterpiece but a cultural epicenter. Inside, you'll find a calendar packed with performances ranging from classical opera to contemporary dance. The grandeur of the theater itself, with its intricate mosaics and lavish interiors, makes attending a performance here a truly immersive experience. Ticket prices vary depending on the performance and seating choice, but even the most modest seats offer a glimpse into the city's thriving arts scene. Attending a show at the Palacio de Bellas Artes is akin to stepping into a living piece of history and artistry.

The Rhythmic Heartbeat of Guadalajara's Mariachi: Traveling west to Guadalajara, you'll encounter the vibrant pulse of mariachi music, deeply rooted in the city's cultural fabric. Plaza de los Mariachis is the epicenter where the soulful strumming of guitars, the harmonious notes of trumpets, and the melodious serenades of violins fill the air. On weekends, this square transforms into a lively stage for local mariachi bands to showcase their talents. The experience is both spontaneous and intimate, as the musicians often engage directly with the audience, making every performance a personal celebration. While there's no fixed entrance fee to the plaza, patrons are encouraged to support the musicians with tips, adding a layer of interaction and support to the musical experience.

The Bohemian Allure of San Miguel de Allende: In the picturesque town of San Miguel de Allende, art takes on a more relaxed and bohemian flair. Known for its colonial charm and vibrant expatriate community, this town is a haven for artists and musicians alike. The San Miguel de Allende Arts Festival, held annually in March, draws artists from around the world. The festival features a range of activities, including art exhibits, workshops, and live music performances. The event is characterized by its eclectic and inclusive spirit, offering something for everyone—from traditional folk performances to avant-garde art installations. While many of the festival's activities are free, some workshops and special events may require a modest fee.

The Coastal Beats of Cancún: On the eastern coast, Cancún offers a different but equally captivating music scene. The city's nightlife is a dynamic blend of beach parties, live music, and world-renowned DJs. Venues like Coco Bongo and The City provide not just a night out but an experience filled with high-energy performances and theatrical shows. These venues are known for their extravagant productions, combining music with acrobatics and live entertainment. Ticket prices for these venues vary, often depending on the night's lineup and show features. Experiencing Cancún's nightlife is like stepping into a vibrant celebration where music and spectacle come together in an unforgettable fusion.

The Cultural Mosaic of Oaxaca: Finally, Oaxaca, with its rich indigenous heritage, offers a unique and deeply cultural music experience. The city's annual

Guelaguetza Festival, held in July, is a grand celebration of Oaxacan culture, featuring traditional music, dance, and folk art. The festival's highlight is its colorful parades and traditional dances, where local communities come together to showcase their cultural pride. Attending the Guelaguetza is more than just observing a performance; it's about immersing yourself in the living traditions of Oaxaca.

11.4 Mexican Cuisine and Cooking Classes

Embarking on a culinary adventure in Mexico is like diving into a vibrant tapestry of flavors, traditions, and stories that have been passed down through generations. Each region of Mexico offers its unique take on the rich and diverse culinary heritage, and participating in local cooking classes provides a profound connection to this cultural mosaic. Here, we explore exceptional Mexican cuisine and cooking classes that will not only enhance your cooking skills but also immerse you in the soul of Mexico's gastronomic delights.

The Heart of Mexican Flavors: In the bustling heart of Mexico City, Casa Jacaranda stands as a beacon of culinary excellence. This cooking school is renowned for its intimate and personalized approach to Mexican cuisine. The classes here are designed to be a deep dive into traditional Mexican cooking, featuring dishes that range from the everyday to the extraordinary. Students have the opportunity to learn the secrets behind iconic dishes such as mole poblano and tamales, guided by experienced chefs who share their passion and expertise. The experience is enriched by the vibrant atmosphere of the Casa, where the cooking environment mirrors the warmth and color of Mexican culture. With prices starting around $150 per class, this culinary journey not only teaches the art of cooking but also offers a rich cultural experience.

Culinary Treasures in Oaxaca: In the picturesque city of Oaxaca, Seasons of My Heart offers a culinary experience that celebrates the rich flavors and ingredients of the region. Founded by renowned chef Susana Trilling, this cooking school provides a deep dive into Oaxacan cuisine, famed for its complex moles and artisanal cheeses. The classes are held in a beautiful colonial-style kitchen surrounded by lush gardens, creating a serene and inspiring environment. Here, you'll learn to craft traditional Oaxacan dishes using locally sourced ingredients and time-honored techniques. The classes, priced around $200, include visits to local markets where you'll discover the vibrant array of spices, vegetables, and herbs that define Oaxacan cuisine.

Coastal Flavors: For those captivated by the flavors of Mexico's Pacific coast, La Cocina de Doña Estela in Puerto Vallarta offers an unforgettable culinary experience. Set in a charming home overlooking the ocean, this cooking school focuses on the seafood-rich cuisine of the region. Led by the esteemed chef Estela Martinez, classes here offer hands-on instruction in preparing dishes such as ceviche and pescado a la talla. The experience is enhanced by the picturesque setting and the opportunity to enjoy meals with a view of the Pacific. With class prices starting at $180, the cost includes not only the cooking lesson but also a full meal, providing a comprehensive taste of Puerto Vallarta's coastal culinary delights.

Maya Gastronomy in Tulum: Tulum, known for its stunning beaches and laid-back vibe, is also home to Coqui Coqui Cooking School, where you can explore the ancient flavors of Maya cuisine. The classes focus on traditional Maya dishes, such as cochinita pibil and sopa de lima, using ingredients native to the Yucatan Peninsula. Students learn to cook in a state-of-the-art kitchen that blends modern conveniences with traditional methods. The price of $250 per class includes a guided tour of local markets and an immersive cooking session that culminates in a feast.

CHAPTER 12
OUTDOOR ADVENTURES

12.1 Hiking Trails and Nature Walks

These trails offers a unique glimpse into Mexico's diverse landscapes, from the rugged grandeur of the Copper Canyon to the mystical beauty of the Monarch Butterfly Biosphere Reserve. Whether you're seeking an adventurous climb or a serene nature walk, Mexico's trails promise an unforgettable experience for every nature enthusiast.

Exploring the Enchanting Trails of the Copper Canyon: In the northern state of Chihuahua, the Copper Canyon, or Barrancas del Cobre, stands as a breathtaking testament to nature's grandeur. This expansive network of canyons, larger and deeper than the Grand Canyon, offers a myriad of hiking trails that cater to every level of adventurer. Among the most prominent routes is the Urique Canyon Trail, a challenging yet rewarding descent that spans approximately 20 miles. The journey takes you through a tapestry of rugged terrain, deep gorges, and verdant forests, presenting an unparalleled opportunity to witness the diverse flora and fauna of the region. Transportation to the Copper Canyon can be an adventure in itself. Visitors typically fly into Chihuahua, with flights costing around $150 to $200 from major US cities. From Chihuahua, travelers can take a scenic train ride on the Chepe Express, with ticket prices ranging from $100 to $250 depending on the class and duration of the trip. The journey provides stunning views of the canyon's dramatic landscape and is an integral part of the overall experience.

The Majestic Journey of the Monarch Butterfly Biosphere Reserve: Located in the central Mexican highlands, the Monarch Butterfly Biosphere Reserve in Michoacán offers a magical hiking experience during the winter months when millions of monarch butterflies converge in the region. The reserve is a UNESCO World Heritage site, known for its stunning butterfly migration. One of the most popular trails is the El Rosario Trail, which stretches for about 6 miles and leads hikers through dense forests of fir and pine, eventually reaching the heart of the butterfly colonies. Reaching the reserve involves a trip to the town of Angangueo. A bus ride from Mexico City to Angangueo costs around $25 to $40, with travel times averaging 3 to 4 hours. From Angangueo, local transportation options include taxis or organized tours that cost approximately $20 to $50, depending on the service and season.

The Mystical Sierra Gorda Biosphere Reserve: In Querétaro, the Sierra Gorda Biosphere Reserve offers a rich and varied hiking experience through one of Mexico's most ecologically diverse regions. The reserve is a haven for biodiversity, with trails such as the Puerta del Cielo Trail showcasing its stunning variety of landscapes. This 10-mile trek meanders through cloud forests, canyons, and oak woodlands, offering dramatic views of the surrounding mountains and valleys. To reach Sierra Gorda, travelers fly into Querétaro, with flights typically costing $100 to $200 from major Mexican cities. From there, it's a 2 to 3-hour drive to the reserve, with car rentals or guided tours available for around $50 to $100 per day.

The Enigmatic Volcanoes of Pico de Orizaba: Pico de Orizaba, or Citlaltépetl, is Mexico's highest peak and a prominent destination for hikers seeking an alpine adventure. Located on the border between Puebla and Veracruz, this dormant volcano offers several trails, with the most challenging being the ascent to the summit. The climb, approximately 16 miles round trip, requires technical climbing skills and appropriate equipment, making it suitable for experienced hikers and mountaineers. Reaching Pico de Orizaba involves flying into Puebla, with flights costing around $100 to $200. From Puebla, travelers can take a bus or arrange private transport to the base camp, with costs ranging from $50 to $150 depending on the service.

The Lush Trails of the Sumidero Canyon: The Sumidero Canyon, located in the state of Chiapas, is a stunning natural formation that offers a range of hiking opportunities along its dramatic cliffs and lush rainforest. The canyon, carved by the Grijalva River, features trails such as the Mirador del Cañon, which offers spectacular views from various vantage points along its 4-mile route. Traveling to Sumidero Canyon typically involves flying into Tuxtla Gutiérrez, with flights costing approximately $100 to $200. From Tuxtla, visitors can take a bus or taxi to the canyon, with transportation costs around $20 to $50.

12.2 Cycling Routes

Cycling in Mexico offers a unique blend of exhilarating adventures and cultural richness. From rugged mountain trails to scenic coastal roads, the country's diverse terrain provides a myriad of routes for cycling enthusiasts. Each route unveils a different aspect of Mexico's natural beauty and vibrant culture, promising an unforgettable experience. Here are five captivating cycling routes across Mexico, each with its own distinctive charm and challenges.

The Copper Canyon Circuit: Embarking on the Copper Canyon Circuit is akin to traversing through a geological marvel. Located in the northern state of Chihuahua, the Copper Canyon, or "Barrancas del Cobre," is a collection of six canyons carved by the Rio Urique. The route begins in the town of Creel, a charming highland settlement. Cyclists will encounter a mix of well-paved and rugged roads as they descend into the canyons and ascend back to higher altitudes. The total distance of this circuit is approximately 300 kilometers, making it a challenging but rewarding endeavor. Expect to traverse diverse landscapes, including pine forests, arid plains, and dramatic cliff edges. The route also provides opportunities to experience the local Tarahumara culture, known for their long-distance running prowess. Transportation costs to reach Creel from Chihuahua City are around $20 to $30 by bus, while local accommodations vary from $50 to $100 per night.

The Yucatán Peninsula Trail: For those seeking a combination of tropical scenery and ancient history, the Yucatán Peninsula Trail is an ideal choice. This route covers about 250 kilometers, winding through the lush landscapes and ancient ruins of Mexico's southeastern region. Starting from the vibrant city of Mérida, cyclists will traverse quiet country roads and scenic coastal paths. Highlights include visits to the archaeological sites of Uxmal and Chichén Itzá, where ancient Mayan architecture stands as a testament to a bygone era. The trail also leads through picturesque cenotes, natural sinkholes filled with crystal-clear water, perfect for a refreshing dip. Transportation costs from Mérida to various trailheads are approximately $15 to $25 by local bus or taxi. Accommodations range from budget hostels at $20 per night to more upscale options at $80 per night.

The Baja California Peninsula Ride: The Baja California Peninsula Ride offers a stunning contrast between desert landscapes and the Pacific Ocean. This route stretches about 400 kilometers from Tijuana to La Paz, providing cyclists with breathtaking coastal views and challenging desert stretches. The ride begins in the bustling border city of Tijuana and continues south along the peninsula, with highlights including the vibrant town of Ensenada and the dramatic cliffs of Cataviña. Cyclists should be prepared for varying weather conditions, with temperatures fluctuating between hot desert days and cooler coastal evenings. The cost of transportation from Tijuana to La Paz by bus or ferry is around $60 to $100, with additional costs for bike transport. Accommodations vary from $30 to $70 per night, depending on the location and amenities.

The Central Highlands Loop: Cycling through Mexico's Central Highlands offers an immersive journey through picturesque colonial towns and lush highland valleys. The route encompasses approximately 200 kilometers and loops through key destinations such as San Miguel de Allende and Guanajuato. Cyclists will navigate a mix of paved roads and scenic trails that meander through rolling hills and vibrant towns. The cultural richness of this route is unparalleled, with opportunities to explore historic sites, local markets, and colorful festivals. The cost of transportation to San Miguel de Allende from Mexico City is about $20 to $40 by bus, with accommodations ranging from $40 to $90 per night in the region.

The Riviera Maya Coastal Route: For a more laid-back yet visually stunning experience, the Riviera Maya Coastal Route is a perfect choice. Spanning roughly 150 kilometers along Mexico's Caribbean coast, this route offers a blend of white-sand beaches, turquoise waters, and vibrant coastal towns. Beginning in the lively city of Cancún, cyclists will traverse through the picturesque towns of Playa del Carmen and Tulum, each offering unique attractions and beachside relaxation. Highlights include visits to Mayan ruins like Tulum and the beautiful beaches of Akumal. Transportation costs from Cancún to Tulum are approximately $15 to $30 by bus, with beachfront accommodations ranging from $50 to $150 per night, depending on the level of luxury desired.

12.3 Water Activities: Snorkeling, Diving, and Surfing

Mexico's enchanting coastlines and crystal-clear waters offer an array of exhilarating water activities that cater to every type of adventurer. From the vibrant underwater worlds ideal for snorkeling and diving to the thrilling waves perfect for surfing, the Mexican waters are a playground for those seeking both relaxation and adrenaline. Here's a detailed guide to experiencing some of the most captivating water activities Mexico has to offer.

Snorkeling in the Riviera Maya: The Riviera Maya, stretching along the Caribbean coast from Cancun to Tulum, is a paradise for snorkelers. The Mesoamerican Barrier Reef, the second-largest reef system in the world, lies just offshore and provides a stunning underwater spectacle. Snorkelers can expect to encounter a vibrant tapestry of marine life, including colorful fish, sea turtles, and even the occasional stingray. Popular snorkeling spots like Cozumel and Akumal are renowned for their clear waters and abundant marine biodiversity. A snorkeling excursion typically includes transportation from your hotel to the dive site, which can cost between $50 and $100 USD per person, depending on the tour package and inclusions such as equipment rental and guided tours. Cozumel is about a 45-minute ferry ride from Playa del Carmen, while Akumal is roughly a 30-minute drive from Tulum. The tour usually lasts around half a day, allowing ample time to enjoy the underwater splendor.

Diving in the Cenotes: For those seeking a more adventurous dive, Mexico's cenotes natural sinkholes filled with fresh groundwater—provide a unique and mesmerizing diving experience. Located primarily in the Yucatan Peninsula, these cenotes offer crystal-clear waters with stunning underwater cave formations. Popular cenotes like Dos Ojos, The Pit, and Gran Cenote each present their own distinct diving experiences. Divers can explore intricate cave systems, swim through underwater tunnels, and observe stalactites and stalagmites in a surreal environment. Diving excursions to the cenotes typically cost between $100 and $150 USD, including equipment rental and transportation from the nearest town. For example, Dos Ojos is about a 20-minute drive from Tulum, while The Pit, known for its deeper, more challenging dives, is approximately a 30-minute drive away. Expect to spend a full day exploring these fascinating underwater landscapes, with dive times varying depending on your skill level and interests.

Surfing in Sayulita: Sayulita, located on the Pacific coast of Nayarit, has emerged as a premier surfing destination in Mexico. Known for its laid-back vibe and consistent waves, Sayulita caters to surfers of all levels, from beginners to experts. The beach break here offers gentle waves ideal for novices, while more advanced surfers can find thrilling swells on the northern end of the beach. Surfing lessons or board rentals in Sayulita generally cost between $40 and $80 USD for a two-hour session. Transportation to Sayulita from Puerto Vallarta, which is about an hour's drive away, costs around $50 USD by taxi or shuttle. Sayulita's surf conditions are best from November to April, with waves that cater to various skill levels, ensuring that surfers can enjoy a rewarding experience regardless of their proficiency.

Kayaking in Lake Chapala: For a serene water activity, kayaking on Lake Chapala, Mexico's largest freshwater lake, offers a peaceful escape amidst picturesque scenery. Located about an hour's drive from Guadalajara, Lake Chapala is ideal for those who prefer tranquil waters and scenic views over more adventurous activities. Paddling through the lake's calm waters, kayakers can enjoy views of the surrounding mountains and lush landscapes, as well as spot local bird species. Kayak rentals are available for around $20 to $40 USD per hour, and guided tours are also an option for those who prefer a more informative experience. The lake's accessibility from Guadalajara makes it a convenient destination for a relaxing day trip. Expect to spend a few hours on the water, soaking in the natural beauty and enjoying the serene environment.

Whale Watching in Baja California: From December to April, the waters off Baja California become a stage for one of nature's most spectacular events: the migration of gray whales. Whale watching tours departing from towns like Loreto and La Paz offer an unforgettable opportunity to witness these majestic creatures as they travel from their feeding grounds in the Arctic to their breeding grounds in the warm waters of Mexico. A whale watching excursion typically costs between $80 and $150 USD, including transportation from your accommodation and a guided tour. The best time for whale watching is from January to March, when the whales are most active. Tours usually last between 3 to 4 hours, providing ample time to observe and appreciate the grandeur of these incredible marine mammals.

12.4 Wildlife Watching: Birds and Marine Life

In Mexico, wildlife watching offers a vibrant tapestry of experiences, each unique and awe-inspiring in its own right. Whether you are marveling at the grandeur of the Great Curassow, swimming with whale sharks, witnessing the Monarch butterfly migration, observing gray whales off Baja California, or tracking the elusive ocelot in the Lacandon Jungle, the country's diverse ecosystems and rich biodiversity promise an unforgettable journey into nature's wonders. Each location offers not just a chance to see wildlife but an opportunity to engage deeply with the natural world, enriching your understanding and appreciation of these magnificent creatures.

Exploring the Yucatán Peninsula: The Yucatán Peninsula, with its lush tropical landscapes and diverse ecosystems, stands as a beacon for birdwatchers and wildlife enthusiasts alike. Among the most sought-after experiences is the chance to witness the magnificent Great Curassow. This large, striking bird, with its vivid plumage and impressive size, is often spotted in the dense rainforests of Calakmul Biosphere Reserve. The reserve itself, covering approximately 723,000 hectares, offers a unique combination of ancient Mayan ruins and rich biodiversity. Visitors can expect a thrilling adventure through the dense jungle, guided by local experts who provide insightful commentary on the region's avian inhabitants. Transportation to Calakmul typically involves a drive from Campeche or Mérida, spanning about 3 to 4 hours, with costs for private transportation ranging from $100 to $150, depending on the vehicle and group size. The journey is well worth it, as the reserve's trails lead to breathtaking views of the Great Curassow amidst the untouched beauty of the rainforest.

Diving with Whale Sharks in the Caribbean Sea: The Caribbean coast of Mexico, particularly around Isla Holbox and Isla Mujeres, offers an unparalleled opportunity to swim with the world's largest fish—the whale shark. These gentle giants migrate to the region from June to September, drawn by the rich plankton blooms in the warm, clear waters. For those keen on experiencing this awe-inspiring encounter, organized tours from Cancun or Playa del Carmen provide access to this marine spectacle. The cost for these tours usually ranges between $200 and $300 per person, covering equipment rental, guide fees, and sometimes a meal. The journey to the dive sites involves a boat trip of about 1 to 2 hours, where visitors are treated to the sight of these magnificent creatures gliding gracefully through the water. Expect to be amazed as you snorkel beside these colossal yet serene beings, a true testament to the wonders of the marine world.

The Monarch Butterfly Migration: Each year, the forests of central Mexico become a living tapestry of orange and black as millions of Monarch butterflies converge in their wintering grounds. The Monarch Butterfly Biosphere Reserve, situated in the mountains of Michoacán, is the epicenter of this incredible migration. The journey from Mexico City to the reserve typically takes about 3 to 4 hours by car, with transportation costs varying between $100 and $150 for a private vehicle. The reserve's trails offer an immersive experience, allowing visitors to witness the butterflies clustering on trees in such vast numbers that they create a mesmerizing visual display. The best time to visit is from late October to early March, when the butterflies are at their peak. This natural phenomenon provides a profound connection with the cyclical patterns of nature, making it a must-see for any wildlife enthusiast.

Baja California: Baja California, with its dramatic coastline and nutrient-rich waters, is a hotspot for marine life observation. One of the region's most compelling attractions is the annual gray whale migration, which occurs between January and March. Observing these majestic creatures as they breach and play in the warm waters off the coast of Baja California Sur is a highlight for many visitors. Tours typically depart from towns like Guerrero Negro or San Ignacio, with costs ranging from $150 to $250 per person. The boat trips usually last about 3 to 4 hours and provide ample opportunities to witness not only the gray whales but also a variety of other marine species, including dolphins and sea lions. The experience is enhanced by knowledgeable guides who share fascinating insights into the lives and behaviors of these ocean giants.

The Ocelot in the Lacandon Jungle: In the remote Lacandon Jungle of Chiapas, the elusive ocelot prowls its natural habitat, making this region a prime destination for wildlife watchers seeking a rare and intimate encounter with one of Mexico's most enigmatic predators. The Lacandon Jungle, part of the Montes Azules Biosphere Reserve, offers a unique combination of guided night hikes and eco-lodges that provide opportunities to spot the ocelot, along with other fascinating wildlife such as jaguars, tapirs, and howler monkeys. Reaching the Lacandon Jungle involves a drive from the city of Palenque, taking around 4 to 5 hours, with transportation costs ranging from $120 to $180. Visitors can expect an immersive experience in one of Mexico's most pristine and biodiverse environments, where the dense forest and diverse wildlife create a truly captivating backdrop for exploration.

12.5 Adventure Sports: Zip-Lining, Rafting, and Rock Climbing

Each of these adventure sports offers a unique way to experience Mexico's diverse landscapes and natural beauty. Whether you're soaring through the jungle, navigating powerful rapids, scaling rugged cliffs, exploring subterranean wonders, or gliding across desert dunes, Mexico's adventure sports promise unforgettable experiences that will leave you exhilarated and inspired.

Zip-Lining Through the Mexican Jungle

Embark on an exhilarating journey through the Mexican jungle with zip-lining, an adventure sport that promises both adrenaline and awe. One of the premier zip-lining experiences can be found in the lush canopy of the Riviera Maya. Here, operators such as Selvatica offer an impressive network of zip lines that stretch across vast distances, allowing adventurers to soar above the dense treetops with breathtaking views of the surrounding tropical forest. The experience combines high-speed thrills with the serene beauty of the jungle, making it an unforgettable excursion. Reaching Riviera Maya is relatively straightforward, with most travelers flying into Cancun, where flights typically cost between $150 and $250 from major US cities. From Cancun, it's a 30 to 45-minute drive to Selvatica, with taxi services or shuttle options available at around $30 to $50. The zip-lining experience itself generally costs between $100 and $150, which includes equipment rental, safety briefings, and guided tours.

White-Water Rafting in Veracruz: For those seeking the ultimate white-water adventure, the rivers of Veracruz offer some of the most thrilling rafting experiences in Mexico. The Río Antigua, with its Class III and IV rapids, provides an exciting challenge for rafting enthusiasts. This river, set against the stunning backdrop of the Sierra Madre Oriental, is renowned for its exhilarating white-water conditions and scenic beauty. Travelers typically fly into Veracruz, with flight costs ranging from $100 to $200. From Veracruz, it's a 2 to 3-hour drive to the river, with transportation options including car rentals or organized tours that cost approximately $50 to $100. The rafting adventure itself generally costs between $80 and $120, covering the necessary equipment, safety briefings, and a guided river experience. Navigating the Río Antigua involves tackling roaring rapids and navigating turbulent waters, which demand both teamwork and skill. The thrill of conquering these powerful waves is tempered by moments of calm, where you can appreciate the lush landscape and crystal-clear waters. The guides, experienced and knowledgeable, ensure safety throughout the journey while sharing insights into the local environment and wildlife. This adventure is perfect for those looking to push their limits and experience the raw power of nature.

Rock Climbing in the Monterrey Sierra: For rock climbing aficionados, the Sierra Madre Oriental near Monterrey offers a climbing paradise with its rugged cliffs and challenging routes. The Parque Nacional Cumbres de Monterrey is renowned for its diverse climbing opportunities, from technical sport climbs to traditional multi-pitch routes. The rock formations here, including the famed El Potrero Chico, provide a range of climbing experiences that cater to both beginners and advanced climbers. Getting to Monterrey involves flying into the city, with flights typically costing between $100 and $200 from major hubs. From Monterrey, it's a 1 to 2-hour drive to the climbing areas, with car rentals or local transportation options available for around $50 to $100. Climbing fees and guide services vary, with costs ranging from $60 to $150 depending on the complexity of the routes and the length of the climb.

Cave Exploration in the Yucatán Peninsula: For a subterranean adventure, the Yucatán Peninsula's cenotes offer a fascinating glimpse into the region's geological wonders. These natural sinkholes, formed by the collapse of limestone bedrock, create a network of underground rivers and caves that are perfect for exploration. Locations such as Cenote Dos Ojos and Cenote Ik Kil are particularly renowned for their stunning underwater landscapes and crystal-clear waters. Traveling to the Yucatán Peninsula typically involves flying into Cancun or Mérida, with flights costing between $150 and $250. From Cancun, it's a 1 to 2-hour drive to the cenotes, with rental cars or local tours available for around $30 to $60. The cost of cenote tours varies, with prices generally ranging from $50 to $100, which includes entry fees, equipment rental, and guided tours.

163

CHAPTER 13

PRACTICAL INFORMATION AND TRAVEL RESOURCES

13.1 Map of Mexico City and Key Destinations

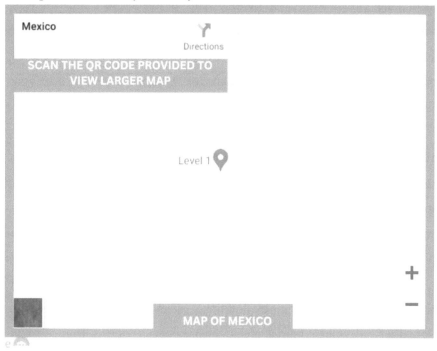

SCAN THE QR CODE WITH A DEVICE TO
VIEW A COMPREHENSIVE AND LARGER
MAP OF MEXICO

Navigating through Mexico, with its vast and diverse landscapes, rich history, and bustling cities, requires a solid understanding of available mapping resources. Whether you are venturing through the sun-drenched beaches of Cancun, the vibrant streets of Mexico City, or the ancient ruins of Oaxaca, having reliable maps and navigation tools at your disposal can greatly enhance your travel experience. This guide will delve into the various methods for accessing both paper and digital maps of Mexico, ensuring that you are well-prepared for your journey.

Understanding Mexico's Tourist Map: For those who appreciate the tactile feel of a paper map, traditional tourist maps of Mexico remain an invaluable resource. These maps are designed with the traveler in mind, highlighting major attractions, cities, landmarks, and essential travel routes. They are often available at travel agencies, airport kiosks, and major hotels across Mexico. These physical maps are particularly useful for quick references and can be carried easily during your explorations. They typically feature detailed information on popular tourist areas, such as the Riviera Maya, the cultural heartlands of Mexico City, and the colonial charm of Guanajuato.

Accessing Digital Maps: Online maps and navigation apps have revolutionized how we explore new destinations. For a comprehensive and interactive experience, digital maps of Mexico offer an array of features that can significantly enhance your travel experience. Popular mapping services like Google Maps, Apple Maps, and MapQuest provide detailed street maps, satellite imagery, and real-time traffic updates. These platforms allow users to zoom in on specific areas, search for points of interest, and even receive turn-by-turn directions. Google Maps, in particular, is a versatile tool that not only provides maps but also integrates with various travel apps, helping you find restaurants, accommodations, and attractions near you. It is crucial to download offline maps if you anticipate being in areas with limited internet connectivity.

Offline Maps: Even in the digital era, having offline access to maps remains essential, especially in remote areas of Mexico where internet coverage might be unreliable. Many travelers opt to download offline maps through apps like Google Maps or maps.me before embarking on their journey. These offline maps provide a safety net for navigating through areas without reliable data services. Additionally, local tourist information centers and travel shops often provide free or inexpensive printed maps that detail popular tourist regions. These maps can be an excellent backup when electronic devices fail or when you simply wish to avoid battery drain during long excursions.

Viewing Comprehensive Maps: To further assist travelers in navigating Mexico with ease, a comprehensive map of Mexico has been included in this guide. For an in-depth view, you can click on the link or scan the QR code provided in this book. This interactive map is designed to offer an extensive overview of Mexico's regions, attractions, and travel routes. It allows for detailed exploration and planning, ensuring that you are well-informed and prepared for your travels.

13.2 Five Days Itinerary

This comprehensive itinerary provides a rich blend of history, culture, and natural beauty, ensuring that every moment of your visit to Mexico is filled with discovery and delight. From the bustling streets of Mexico City to the serene beaches of Tulum, each day offers a new adventure, immersing you in the heart and soul of this fascinating country.

Day One: Arrival and Exploration of Mexico City

Upon arrival in Mexico City, the vibrant capital, you will immediately feel the pulse of one of the largest and most dynamic cities in the world. Begin your adventure with a visit to the historic center, Zócalo, where the city's rich past converges with its bustling present. This grand square is flanked by iconic landmarks such as the Metropolitan Cathedral, the largest in the Americas, and the National Palace, home to the famous murals by Diego Rivera. Take a leisurely stroll through these historic sites, absorbing the architectural beauty and the stories they tell. Next, make your way to the nearby Templo Mayor, an ancient Aztec temple complex that offers a fascinating glimpse into pre-Hispanic history. The adjacent museum houses a remarkable collection of artifacts that further illuminate the Aztec civilization. After soaking in the history, head to Alameda Central, a picturesque park perfect for a relaxing walk or a refreshing break.

Day Two: Teotihuacan and the Basilica of Our Lady of Guadalupe

On your second day, venture outside the city to the ancient city of Teotihuacan, one of the most significant archaeological sites in Mexico. Known as the "City of the Gods," Teotihuacan was once a thriving metropolis and is now famous for its impressive pyramids. Climb the Pyramid of the Sun and the Pyramid of the Moon for breathtaking views of the site and the surrounding landscape. Wander along the Avenue of the Dead, exploring the various temples and palaces that reveal the grandeur of this ancient civilization. After returning to Mexico City, make a stop at the Basilica of Our Lady of Guadalupe, one of the most important pilgrimage sites in the world. This sacred site attracts millions of visitors each year and offers a deep insight into the spiritual heart of Mexico. The modern basilica, along with the old basilica and the chapel on Tepeyac Hill, provide a serene setting for reflection and admiration.

Day Three: Puebla and Cholula

Embark on a day trip to the charming city of Puebla, known for its colonial architecture, vibrant tiles, and culinary delights. Begin your exploration at the Zócalo, the central square surrounded by stunning buildings like the Puebla Cathedral and the Palafoxiana Library, the oldest public library in the Americas.

Stroll through the streets, admiring the beautifully tiled facades and stopping by the local markets to sample regional specialties such as mole poblano and chiles en nogada. In the afternoon, visit the nearby town of Cholula, home to the Great Pyramid of Cholula, the largest pyramid by volume in the world. Climb to the top for panoramic views and explore the tunnels beneath to understand its extensive history. The Iglesia de Nuestra Señora de los Remedios, perched atop the pyramid, adds a unique blend of ancient and colonial history.

Day Four: Oaxaca City and Monte Albán

Fly to Oaxaca City, a UNESCO World Heritage site renowned for its well-preserved colonial architecture, vibrant culture, and rich traditions. Start your day at the Zócalo, the lively main square surrounded by historical buildings and bustling with activity. Visit the Santo Domingo Church and its adjoining cultural center, which offers insights into Oaxaca's history and culture. After exploring the city, take a short trip to Monte Albán, one of the most important archaeological sites in Mesoamerica. Situated on a hilltop with stunning views of the valley, Monte Albán was once the center of the Zapotec civilization. Wander through the expansive ruins, including the Great Plaza, ball courts, and intricate carvings that depict the ancient way of life.

Day Five: Beaches of Tulum and Riviera Maya

Conclude your Mexican adventure with a relaxing day on the pristine beaches of Tulum and the Riviera Maya. Fly to Cancún and head south to Tulum, where you can explore the ancient Mayan ruins overlooking the Caribbean Sea. The Tulum Ruins are unique for their picturesque setting and well-preserved structures, providing a striking contrast between history and natural beauty. Spend the rest of the day enjoying the white sandy beaches and crystal-clear waters of the Riviera Maya. Whether you choose to relax under a palm tree, snorkel in the vibrant coral reefs, or indulge in water sports, this region offers a perfect blend of relaxation and adventure. Visit a cenote, a natural sinkhole filled with freshwater, for a refreshing swim in a unique and serene setting.

13.3 Safety Tips and Emergency Contacts

Singapore is often hailed as one of the safest cities in the world, renowned for its low crime rates and efficient law enforcement. However, visitors should still be mindful of certain safety measures to ensure a smooth and secure experience. Understanding the local context and adhering to recommended practices can significantly enhance your safety and peace of mind while exploring this vibrant city-state.

General Safety Practices: As with any travel destination, it is wise to exercise common sense and stay alert. Singapore's public areas, including its bustling streets and well-maintained parks, are generally safe at all hours. However, it is advisable to avoid isolated areas after dark. Personal belongings should always be kept close, especially in crowded places such as shopping malls, markets, and public transport hubs. While pickpocketing is rare, it is not entirely unheard of, so keeping your valuables secure is a prudent measure.

Health and Medical Services: Singapore boasts a world-class healthcare system with numerous hospitals, clinics, and pharmacies easily accessible throughout the city. For minor ailments, over-the-counter medication is readily available at pharmacies. However, it is recommended to carry a basic first aid kit with personal medication you might need. In the event of a medical emergency, the universal emergency number 995 can be dialed for an ambulance. Public hospitals such as Singapore General Hospital and Tan Tock Seng Hospital offer excellent emergency services. Travel insurance is highly recommended to cover any potential medical expenses during your stay.

Local Laws and Regulations: Singapore is known for its strict laws and regulations, which contribute significantly to its overall safety. Visitors should familiarize themselves with local laws to avoid unintentional violations. Acts such as littering, smoking in prohibited areas, and jaywalking can result in substantial fines. Additionally, drug-related offenses carry severe penalties, including the death penalty for trafficking. Chewing gum is also regulated; while it is not illegal to chew gum, importing and selling gum (except for medical purposes) is prohibited. Smoking is banned in all indoor public places and within a certain distance from building entrances. Designated smoking areas are clearly marked, and it is essential to adhere to these restrictions to avoid fines.

Natural Disasters and Environmental Safety: Singapore is relatively free from natural disasters such as earthquakes and hurricanes. However, the city occasionally experiences haze from forest fires in neighboring countries. During haze periods, the National Environment Agency (NEA) provides regular updates on air quality, and it is advisable to stay indoors and use air purifiers if the air quality index rises to unhealthy levels.

Emergency Contacts and Assistance: Knowing key emergency contacts can be invaluable in times of need. The primary emergency number for police, fire, and ambulance services is 999. For non-emergency medical assistance, you can contact the Ministry of Health's 24-hour hotline at 1800-225-4122. The Singapore Tourism Board also provides a visitor helpline at 1800-736-2000, offering assistance with tourist-related queries and emergencies.

Staying Connected and Informed: Staying connected with local news and updates is crucial for safety. The Singapore Civil Defence Force (SCDF) and the Singapore Police Force (SPF) provide timely updates through their websites and social media channels.

13.4 Shopping and Souvenirs

Directions from Mexico to Bodega Malazzo, Lago Iseo, Anáhuac I Sección, Mexico City, CDMX, Mexico

A
Mexico

B
La Ciudadela, Balderas, Colonia Centro, Centro, Mexico City, CDMX, Mexico

D
Mercado de Artesanías, General Ignacio Zaragoza, OAX_RE_BENITO JUAREZ, Centro, Oaxaca, Mexico

C
La Casa de las Sirenas, República de Guatemala, Historic center of Mexico City, Centro, Mexico City, CDMX, Mexico

E
Bodega Malazzo, Lago Iseo, Anahuac I Seccion, Mexico City, CDMX, Mexico

Mexico, with its rich cultural heritage and vibrant local arts, offers a unique shopping experience that blends tradition with modernity. For visitors seeking distinctive souvenirs and boutique finds, the country boasts a variety of shopping venues. Each location has its own charm and specialty, promising a memorable shopping experience. Here's a look at exceptional shopping spots in Mexico, each offering its own unique selection of goods and a glimpse into the local culture.

La Ciudadela Market: La Ciudadela Market is a treasure trove for those seeking authentic Mexican crafts and souvenirs. Located at Balderas 6, Centro Histórico, this bustling market is renowned for its diverse selection of handcrafted goods. Here, visitors can explore an array of traditional Mexican items such as vibrant textiles, intricate pottery, colorful talavera tiles, and handwoven baskets. Prices vary widely depending on the item and craftsmanship, ranging from as little as $10 for smaller souvenirs to several hundred dollars for larger, more intricate pieces. The market operates from 10 AM to 6 PM daily, providing ample time to wander through its vibrant stalls. To reach La Ciudadela Market, visitors can take the Metro to Balderas Station, which is conveniently located nearby. From there, it's a short walk to the market entrance. The lively atmosphere and the variety of goods make it a must-visit for anyone wanting to take home a piece of Mexican culture.

Casa de las Sirenas: For a more boutique shopping experience, Casa de las Sirenas in Mexico City's historic center offers a curated selection of high-quality Mexican arts and crafts. Situated at Donceles 99, this charming store specializes in artisanal jewelry, handcrafted leather goods, and traditional Mexican art. The store prides itself on offering unique, high-end items that reflect the rich heritage of Mexico. Prices here are generally higher, with jewelry pieces starting around $50 and leather goods from $100 upwards. Casa de las Sirenas is open from 11 AM to 7 PM on weekdays and 10 AM to 8 PM on weekends. It's easily accessible by public transportation, with the closest Metro station being Bellas Artes. From there, a short walk will lead visitors to the store's elegant facade. The boutique's refined selection and welcoming atmosphere make it a perfect stop for those in search of a sophisticated souvenir.

Antigüedades Sánchez: In the vibrant city of Guadalajara, Antigüedades Sánchez stands out for its impressive collection of antiques and vintage items. Located at Avenida de la Reforma 1234, this antique store offers a fascinating array of historical artifacts, vintage furniture, and collectible items. Whether you're in search of old Mexican coins, colonial-era furniture, or classic porcelain pieces, Antigüedades Sánchez provides a captivating glimpse into Mexico's past. Prices vary significantly, with small collectibles starting at $30 and larger furniture pieces costing several thousand dollars. The store operates from 10 AM to 5 PM Tuesday through Saturday, and closed on Sundays. Visitors can reach Antigüedades Sánchez via local taxis or ride-sharing services, as public transportation options may be limited. The shop's extensive collection and knowledgeable staff offer a unique shopping experience for antique enthusiasts.

Mercado de Artesanías de Oaxaca: For those visiting Oaxaca, the Mercado de Artesanías is a vibrant marketplace brimming with traditional crafts and local specialties. Located at Av. 20 de Noviembre 8, this market features a wide variety of Oaxacan crafts, including handwoven rugs, intricate wood carvings, and vibrant textiles. Prices range from modestly priced trinkets for $10 to elaborate handwoven rugs costing several hundred dollars. The market also offers a range of local foods and drinks, adding to the sensory experience.

La Bodega de los Sabores: In the coastal city of Cancun, La Bodega de los Sabores offers a delightful shopping experience focused on local gourmet products and artisanal goods. Located at Blvd. Kukulcán 22, this store is renowned for its selection of Mexican spices, gourmet salsas, and handcrafted chocolates. It's an ideal spot for foodies looking to take home a taste of Mexico. Prices are generally affordable, with spice packs starting around $10 and gourmet chocolates around $20. La Bodega de los Sabores is open from 9 AM to 8 PM daily, making it convenient for visitors to stop by at their leisure. The store is easily accessible by local transport or taxi, situated conveniently along the main tourist strip. The store's emphasis on quality and local flavors provides a unique shopping experience that highlights Mexico's culinary delights.

13.5 Useful Websites, Mobile Apps and Online Resources

Using these digital tools can significantly enhance your Singapore travel experience. The STB website lays a solid foundation for planning, while MyTransport.SG ensures smooth navigation through public transport. Chope simplifies dining reservations, and Grab offers versatile transportation and delivery services. The Visit Singapore Travel Guide app provides curated content and personalized itineraries. Together, these resources make exploring Singapore convenient, enriching, and enjoyable, ensuring a memorable visit.

Singapore Tourism Board Official Website: The Singapore Tourism Board (STB) website is an essential resource for all visitors. It offers a wealth of information on attractions, events, accommodations, and practical travel tips. Interactive maps and downloadable brochures enhance trip planning, providing insights into local customs, transportation, and dining options. This site is a comprehensive guide for tailoring your Singapore adventure.

MyTransport.SG Mobile App: Navigating Singapore's efficient public transport system is effortless with the MyTransport.SG app. It provides real-time updates on buses, MRT services, and road conditions, along with route planning and service disruption alerts. The app's features extend to taxi bookings, cycling routes, and parking information, making it a versatile tool for all transport needs.

Chope Restaurant Reservation Platform: Chope is a must-have for food enthusiasts looking to explore Singapore's diverse culinary scene. This platform, available as both a website and an app, allows users to discover and book tables at a variety of restaurants. Featuring reviews, menus, and exclusive deals, Chope makes dining planning easy and convenient, ensuring you can enjoy popular spots without long waits.

Grab: Grab is a leading ride-hailing app in Southeast Asia, offering various transportation options, including taxis, private cars, and shared rides. The app's transparent pricing and cashless payments add convenience. Additionally, Grab provides food delivery services, allowing you to savor Singapore's cuisine from anywhere. Its rewards program offers discounts and benefits, enhancing the overall experience.

Visit Singapore Travel Guide: The Visit Singapore Travel Guide app, developed by the STB, is a digital companion for exploring the city. It offers curated content on attractions, events, and activities tailored to your interests. Users can create personalized itineraries and navigate easily with integrated maps. The app also highlights seasonal festivals and local events, ensuring you experience the best of Singapore.

13.6 Internet Access and Connectivity

Traveling to Mexico offers the allure of vibrant cities, stunning landscapes, and rich culture, but staying connected is essential to fully enjoy and navigate your visit. The country has made significant strides in internet access and connectivity, ensuring that visitors can remain in touch, navigate their surroundings, and access essential services seamlessly. Understanding the various options for internet connectivity will enhance your travel experience and keep you connected throughout your journey.

Wi-Fi Access Across Mexico: Mexico boasts extensive Wi-Fi coverage, particularly in urban areas, tourist hotspots, and hospitality venues. Major cities like Mexico City, Guadalajara, and Monterrey have numerous public Wi-Fi spots available in parks, squares, and cafes. Most hotels, restaurants, and shopping centers offer free Wi-Fi for their patrons, making it relatively easy to stay connected. For travelers in more remote areas or smaller towns, access may be less widespread, so it is advisable to confirm Wi-Fi availability before making travel plans.

SIM Cards and Mobile Data: Purchasing a local SIM card is an effective way to stay connected while traveling through Mexico. Major Mexican mobile carriers, such as Telcel, Movistar, and AT&T, offer a variety of prepaid SIM card options that cater to different data needs and durations of stay. These SIM cards can be easily acquired at airports, convenience stores, and carrier stores throughout the country. The SIM cards provide not only data but also local call and text services, allowing for seamless communication.

13.7 Visitor Centers and Tourist Assistance
Visitor centers and tourist assistance services are pivotal for navigating the vibrant and diverse regions of Mexico. These centers provide essential support, offering a wealth of information and resources that help travelers maximize their experience while ensuring a smooth and enjoyable visit. Understanding the role and offerings of these centers can significantly enhance your journey through this captivating country.

Cancun Tourist Information Center: The Cancun Tourist Information Center is a cornerstone for visitors exploring one of Mexico's most popular resort destinations. Located strategically in Cancun's bustling Hotel Zone, this center is designed to cater to the needs of tourists looking to explore the city's renowned beaches, lively nightlife, and nearby attractions. The center provides a range of services including detailed maps of the area, brochures on local attractions, and up-to-date information on events and activities.

Mexico City Tourism Office: In the sprawling metropolis of Mexico City, the Mexico City Tourism Office is an essential resource for anyone looking to delve into the rich cultural and historical offerings of the capital. This office provides comprehensive information on a wide range of attractions, including historical landmarks, museums, and art galleries.

Merida Tourist Information Center: In the heart of the Yucatan Peninsula, the Merida Tourist Information Center serves as a gateway to exploring the region's unique blend of Mayan heritage and colonial architecture. Located centrally in Merida, the center offers a wealth of information on nearby archaeological sites such as Chichen Itza and Uxmal. Visitors can obtain detailed brochures, maps, and expert advice on how to make the most of their visit to the Yucatan. The

Puerto Vallarta Visitor Center: The Puerto Vallarta Visitor Center is a crucial resource for travelers exploring this picturesque coastal city. Located in the city center, the visitor center offers comprehensive support for navigating the city's many attractions, from its stunning beaches to its vibrant cultural scene.

CONCLUSION AND RECOMMENDATIONS

As we reach the end of our journey through Mexico in this comprehensive travel guide, it's clear that this enchanting country is more than just a destination—it's an invitation to experience a vibrant tapestry of cultures, landscapes, and histories. From the sun-drenched beaches of Cancun to the bustling streets of Mexico City, and from the ancient ruins of the Yucatan Peninsula to the colonial charm of Guadalajara, Mexico offers a kaleidoscope of experiences that promise to captivate and inspire. To make the most of your journey, here are some insider tips that will help you uncover the hidden gems of Mexico and navigate its myriad experiences with ease:

Embrace Local Flavors and Street Food: Mexican cuisine is celebrated worldwide, but nothing compares to the authenticity of local street food. Venture beyond the tourist spots and explore local markets and street vendors. Try the tacos al pastor in Mexico City, savor the fresh seafood in Puerto Vallarta, and don't miss out on the delicious tamales and mole in Oaxaca. These culinary delights are not just meals but an integral part of the Mexican cultural experience.

Learn Basic Spanish Phrases: While many Mexicans in tourist areas speak English, knowing a few basic Spanish phrases can enhance your experience and endear you to locals. Simple greetings, thank-yous, and questions will help you navigate interactions more smoothly and show respect for the local culture. The effort to communicate in Spanish is often appreciated and can lead to more authentic and enriching encounters.

Explore Beyond the Tourist Trails: Mexico is brimming with hidden treasures that lie off the beaten path. Consider visiting smaller towns and rural areas to experience the authentic Mexican lifestyle. Places like Valle de Bravo offer serene lakeside views and charming local markets, while the highlands of Chiapas provide an opportunity to see traditional indigenous cultures and breathtaking natural beauty. These off-the-beaten-path destinations provide a more intimate glimpse into the heart of Mexico.

Stay Hydrated and Use Sunscreen: Mexico's varied climates can be quite intense, especially during the summer months. Whether you're exploring the arid deserts or sunbathing on the Caribbean coast, it's crucial to stay hydrated and apply sunscreen regularly. This simple precaution will help you stay comfortable and enjoy your travels without the discomfort of dehydration or sunburn.

Respect Local Customs and Traditions: Each region of Mexico has its own customs and traditions. When visiting sacred sites or participating in local festivals, it's important to be mindful of and respect local customs. Dress modestly when visiting religious sites, and approach traditional ceremonies with reverence. This respect not only enriches your travel experience but also fosters positive interactions with local communities.

Mexico's allure lies in its ability to offer something for every type of traveler. Whether you're drawn to its rich history, vibrant culture, breathtaking landscapes, or culinary delights, Mexico promises an experience that is as diverse as it is unforgettable. As you prepare for your adventure, let these insider tips guide you toward a journey that is not only enjoyable but deeply memorable. Embrace the spirit of Mexico with an open heart and a curious mind, and you'll find yourself captivated by the beauty, warmth, and richness of this extraordinary country. Your Mexican adventure awaits, and it's bound to be a journey filled with wonder, discovery, and cherished memories.

Made in United States
Troutdale, OR
12/23/2024

27216716R00104